Zero to Mastery in
CYBER SECURITY

Zero to Mastery in
CYBER SECURITY

DR. R.K. JAIN

AN ISO 9001:2008 CERTIFIED COMPANY

Vayu Education of India

2/25, Ansari Road, Darya Ganj, New Delhi-110 002

Copyright © Vayu Education of India

First Edition: 2022

All rights reserved. No part of this publication may be reproduced, stored in a retrieval system, or transmitted, in any form or by any means, electronic, mechanical, photocopying, recording or otherwise, without the prior permission of the copyright owners.

DISCLAIMER

Errors, if any, are purely unintentional and readers are requested to communicate such errors to the publisher to avoid discrepancies in future.

Published by:

AN ISO 9001:2008 CERTIFIED COMPANY

VAYU EDUCATION OF INDIA

2/25, ANSARI ROAD, DARYA GANJ, NEW DELHI-110 002
PH.: 011-41564440, MOB. 09910115201

Contents

SPECIAL BONUS!

Want These 3 Bonus Books for free?

Get <u>FREE</u>, unlimited access to these and all of our new books by joining our community!

SCAN w/ your camera TO JOIN!

OR Visit

freebie.kartbucket.com

Chapter **1**

INFORMATION SYSTEM

In this age of information, almost all fields of endeavor such as education, manufacturing, research, games, entertainment, and business treat information systems as a need. Indeed, every activity in our daily life today requires people to get involved in the use of information systems.

First, to understand the system, there is a need to understand the three concepts.

1. Data.
2. Process.
3. Information.
4. System.

Data

Data is a raw material. Data refers to the raw facts on any thing or entities like student names, courses and marks. The raw data that has not yet been provided can be processed to become more useful information.

For example:

- In addition of two numbers, we need more than one data. Such as a (a=2) and b (b=4).
- In a class, student name, roll number, age and their marks are the data.

Process

Process or procedure explains the activities performed by users. Process is a guide consisting of orderly steps, which need to be implemented in order to get a certain decision on a certain matter.

Information

The data after processing is called information.

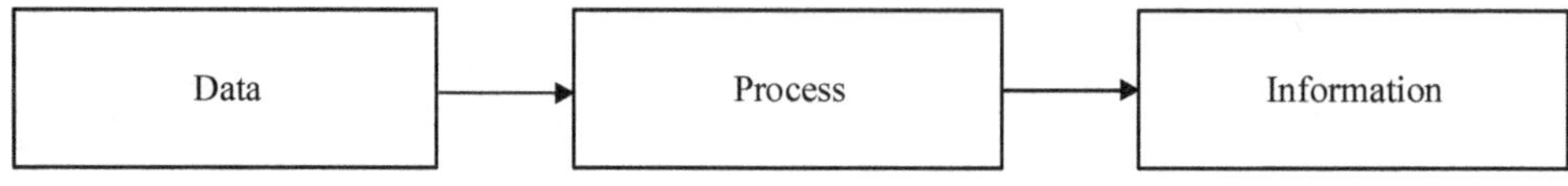

Fig. 1.1

Information is an organized, meaningful and useful interpretation of data such as a company performances or a student's academic performance. Information systems change data after perform some process into information, which is useful and capable of giving a certain meaning to its users.

For example: - In addition of two number the data (Raw material) is a (a=2)and b (b=4) and after addition of these data the result is c (c=6). The information c (c=6) is getting after the processing over the data.

In a class, student name, roll number, age and their marks are the data and performing some process like mathematical calculation (average formula). We get the information about the class. Such as the class's performance.

Hardware

Hardware is the physical component of the computer which can be touch and feel by the user.

These component include the following-

1. Input Devices.   2. Output Devices   3. Storage Devices.

Software

Computer software, or just **software**, is a collection of computer programs and related data that provides the instructions for telling a computer what to do and how to do it.

The program is the sequence of instruction that are designed to accomplish a particular task. The collection of programs that are designed for a specific purpose is called the software.

System

A system is simply a group of activities and elements and all activities are executed in a manner to achieve the specific task or purpose.

Information System

The information system is the collection of hardware and software and designed to achieve the specific task. Information system helps people for making the business decisions.

In the current era of globalization, the success of a business depends on the information system. Many organizations today use information systems to offer services with greater satisfaction to customers, to access a wider range of information, to handle business changes at a greater speed, and to increase the productivity of workers. Based on a number of researches, an effective information system should be able to exceed customer expectations and fulfill business needs.

Types of Information System

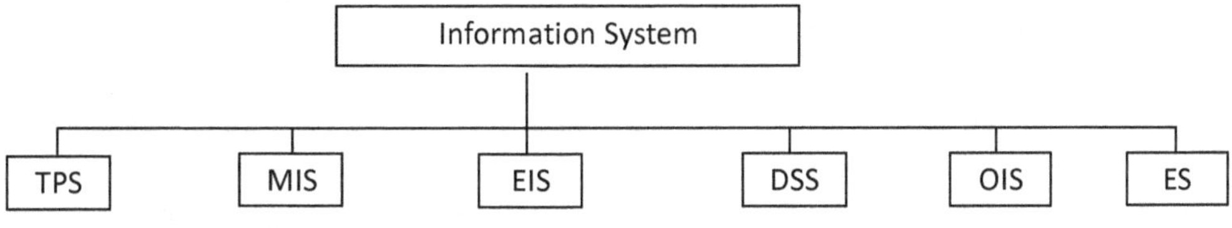

Fig. 1.2

Transaction Processing System (TPS)

- TPS can access information about all transactions related to the organization.
- Transactions occur whenever there exist activities involving sales order processing, accounts receivable, accounts payable, inventory and ordering as well as payroll.
- These transactions involve credit and debit in the company ledger account.
- The output from this transaction is the account statement, which is used to generate financial reports.
- TPS now uses the latest technology which uses the E-commerce concept. This is a new challenge in the field of transaction processing which begins to shift to the on-line transaction processing system.

Management Information System (MIS)

- This system will take the information that has been extracted form
- TPS and generate reports which are required by the management for planning and controlling a Company's business.
- This system is capable of fulfilling the needs of management in acquiring the information that:

(a) is brief and useful.

(b) can be obtained and processed at the right time to make a decision.

Executive Information System (EIS)

- A decision support system specifically used by the executive management in making strategic decisions.

- It is a tool that provides online access directly to the relevant information, in the format that is useful and can be browsed.

- Relevant information is timely, precise and useful in business aspects, according to the interest of certain managers.

- Useful format, and can be browsed easily; will mean that the system has been specially built for the use of individuals who have little time to spare, are less skilful in using the keyboard and less experienced with computers.

- This system can be surfed easily so that managers can identify strategic issues and can then explore information for getting the sources about those issues.

- It is also an information system that combines the features of information reporting system and decision support system. It focuses on fulfilling the strategic information needs of the top management.

Decision Support System (DSS)

- The main focus of this information system is for the effectiveness of the manager in analyzing the information and making a decision.

- It is used for handling decisions that are not structured, i.e. decisions which are made when an emergency happens.

- This system uses a database management system, query language, financial modeling, electronic spread sheet, statistical analysis program, report generator or graphic software for supplying the information needed.

Office Information System (OIS)

- Office automation is wider than word processing and form processing.

- This information system covers activities in the office, which can improve work flow and communication among workers, whether inside or outside the office.

- The focus of this system is on the collection of information for who ever needs it.

- The functions of this system are word processing, e-mails, work group programming, work group scheduling, facsimile processing, e-document, imaging and management of work flow.

Expert System (ES)

- It is a program that produces a decision which is almost similar to decisions made by an expert in a certain discipline.

- This information system can imitate the way humans think and consider in making a decision.

- An expert system will combine the use of knowledge, facts and techniques to make a decision.

- An expert can always give a certain decision which is accurate as well as ensuring maximum benefit to all the people concerned. Unfortunately, the sources for expert services are limited.

- Realizing the high value of knowledge and the expertise owned by the expert, researchers have tried to transfer and save in the computers the knowledge and expertise owned by the experts.

- Through this work, the expert system is made.

Information System Participants / Individuals in IS

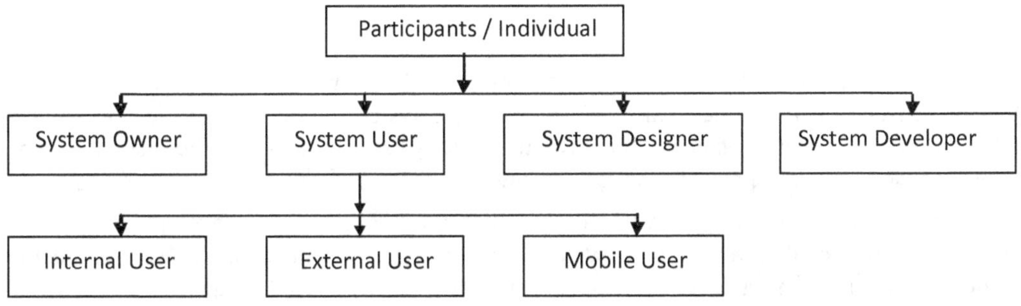

Fig. 1.3

System Owner

The systems owner bears the cost of system development and maintenance. He has the right over the system, determines the interest over the system and determines the policies over its use. The system owner is also responsible for system justification and system acceptance. In certain situations, the system owner is also a system user.

System owners always think of the return value, which can be obtained by developing the information system. This return is valued from various aspects such as:

- What are the benefits of the system?

- What are the mission and objectives?

- What is the cost of developing the system?

- What is the cost of operating the system?

- Can the investment pay back the capital?

System Designer

Systems designers are experts in the technical field who would design a system for fulfilling the needs of users. They are responsible for manipulating the needs of business users and the constraints in technical solutions. They design computer files, databases, input, output, screen, networks, and programs that can fulfill the needs of system users. They are also responsible for integrating the technical solutions into the daily business environment.

Systems designers understand the technological environment better when compared to systems owners and systems users. They always provide alternatives and design systems based on technological constraints at that time. Now, systems designers give more attention to technical experts such as:

- Database designers who provide focus on the data.
- Programmers and software engineers who provide focus on the process.
- Systems integrators who provide focus on the system interfaces.
- Telecommunication and network experts who provide focus on the geographic locations.

System Developer

Systems developers are the experts in the technical field who would develop, test and produce a system, which can operate successfully. They build the system components based on the design specifications of the system designers. In many situations, system designers are the system developers. They use technology to develop information systems.

Among the individuals who get involved directly in information system development, you maybe ask what is the role of the systems analyst? In actual fact, the systems analysts are really acting as facilitators for information systems development. The system analyst has the expertise that is owned by all the above individuals. They should feel comfortable with the views of all the individuals mentioned above. For the systems owners and users, the systems analyst should develop and update their views. The duty of the systems analyst is to ensure that the technical knowledge of systems designers and developers are consistent with the current business needs.

System User

The system user is an individual who uses the system for producing something, or uses the system to help him in his daily jobs. Directly, users are the ones who get the benefits from the system that has been developed. Besides being the initiators for the new information system request, users also determine:

- The problems to be solved.
- Opportunities to be exploited.
- The needs to be fulfilled.
- Business constraints to be overcome by the system.
- Whether the information system that has been developed is easy or difficult to use.

Internal User

Employees who work in the company to develop the information system. Internal users constitute the highest percentage among those who use the said system. They include the support and administrative staff, the technical and professional staff, supervisors, the management and the executives.

External User

The information system can no connect the system to other individuals as users of the system.

Due to global competition, businesses are redesigned to enable connectivity with other organizations, partners, suppliers, customers and end users.

As an example, you need not fill up any form to apply for entry into OUM. With the information system provided by OUM, you just need to go to the OUM website, fill up the application form online, and send the form online. Now, the facility is provided, but in future it may be necessary to change our way of life.

Development of Information System

An information system can be developed in phases and the order in which phases are to be executed. Each phase produces deliverables required by the next phase in the life cycles of the Information System.

There are following phases in the development of the Information System.

1.   Requirement gathering and analysis: Business requirements are gathered in this phase. The main focus in this phase on the requirements like:

Who is going to use the system?

How will they use the system?

What data should be input into the system?

What data should be output by the system?

These are the general questions that get answered during the requirement gathering phase. Requirement specification document is created which serves the purpose of guideline for the next phase of the development of Information System.

2.   Design: In this phase the system design is prepared from the requirement specifications which were studied in the first phase. System design helps in specifying hardware and system requirements and also helps in defining overall architecture. The system design specification serve as input for the next phase of the Information system.

3.   Implementation / coding: On receiving system design documents, the work is divided into modules/ units and actual coding is started. This is longest phase of the development of information system.

4. Testing: After the code is developed it is tested against the requirements to make sure that the product is actually solving the needs addressed and gathered during the requirement phase. Testing is the activity performed to check the quality of the information system against defect. In testing phase the system is testing with intent of finding errors.

5. Deployment: After successful testing the product is delivered / deployed to the customer for their use .

6. Maintenance: Once, when the customers start using the developed system then the actual problems up and needs to be solved from time to time. This process where the care is taken for the developed product is known as maintenance.

Questions

Q.1. What is information system and give the components of information system?

Q.2. Define information system and what are the types of information system?

Q.3. Write a short notes of the following:

    (*i*)   Management Information System

    (*ii*)   Executive Information System

    (*iii*)   Decision Support system

    (*iv*)   Expert System

Q.4. Explain in details information system participants?

Q.5. Explain in details development of information system?

Q.6. What is Information System? How does information system relate to business and help them?

INFORMATION SECURITY

According to the UK Government, Information security is: **"The practice of ensuring information is only read, heard, changed, broadcast and otherwise used by people who have the right to do so."** (Source: UK Online for Business)

Information systems need to be secure if they are to be reliable. Since many businesses are critically reliant on their information systems for key business processes (e.g. websites, production scheduling, transaction processing), security can be seen to be a very important area for management to get right.

Need for Information Security

Computer security is the process of preventing and detecting unauthorized use of your computer. Prevention measures help you to stop unauthorized users from accessing any part of your computer system. Detection helps you to determine whether or not someone attempted to break into your system, if they were successful, and what they may have done.

Security Requirements

Needs for information systems security and trust can be formulated in terms of several major requirements:

- **Data confidentiality** - controlling who gets to read information in order to keep

   sensitive information from being disclosed to unauthorized recipients - e.g.,

   preventing the   sclosure of classified information to an adversary.

- **Data integrity** - assuring that information and programs are changed, altered, or modified only in a specified and authorized manner - e.g., preventing an adversary from modifying orders given to combat units so as to shape battlefield events to his advantage.

- **System availability** - assuring that authorized users have continued and timely access to information and resources - e.g., preventing an adversary from flooding a network with bogus traffic that delays legitimate traffic such as that containing new orders from being transmitted.

- **System configuration**- assuring that the configuration of a system or a network is changed only in accordance with established security guidelines and only by authorized users.

- **Authentication** - ascertaining that the identity claimed by a party is indeed the identity of that party.Authentication is generally based on what a party knows (e.g., a password), what a party has (e.g., hardware computer-readable token), or what a party is (e.g., a fingerprint).

- **Authorization** - granting of permission to a party to perform a given action (or set of actions)

- **Auditing** - recording each operation that is invoked along with the identity of the subject performing it and the object acted upon (as well as later examining these records).

- **Non-repudiation** - the use of a digital signature procedure affirming both the integrity of a given message and the identity of its creator to protect against a subseqeuent attempt to deny authenticity.

Information System threats / attacks

There are mainly two types of threats in Information System.

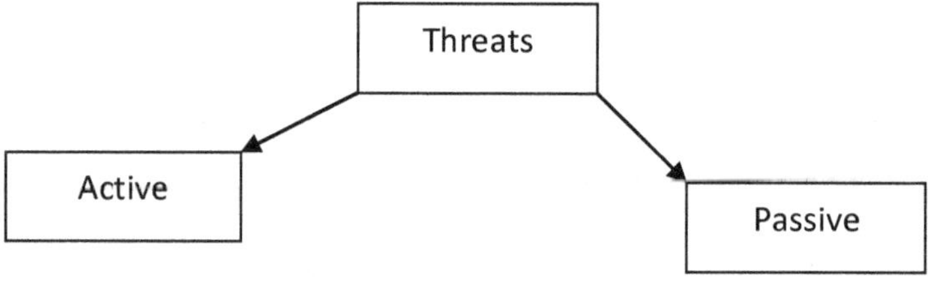

Fig. 2.1

Passive Threats

Security threats are in the nature of monitoring of transmission of many types. The goal of this attack or the hacker doing the attack is to gain information or the information that is being transmitted in the message to gain a edge of other party.

Passive attacks are very hard to detect because they do not damaged or changed the information. So you can not tell they have been attacked.

Types of Passive Threats

There are main two types of passive attack.

1. Release of message content: It is easy to grasp just from it name and what it does it easily figureout also. In this type of passive attack a mail message, phone call any transferred message pretty much of sensitive information that would be intercepted.

2. Traffic analysis: Traffic analysis is little more complicated and it is very subtle and hard to detect. It would be like this if we had a way to hide the information on a message and the hacker still viewed the information'

Active threats

Active threats attempt to change the system it is attacking. Active threats always involve a modification of data stream. There are four main categories of attacks –

- **Masquerade:** - It is a term used when an attacking network personates a valid device. It is the ideal approach. If an attacker wants to remain undetected. If the device can successfully fool the target network into validating it as an authorized device the attacker gets all the access rights that the authorized device stabilized during log on.

- **Replay:** - Replay attack capture information sent by an unwary client and later attempts to reuse, replay that information in order to gain access to protected data.

- **Modification:** - It changes the information included in messages being processed between two of more entities.

- **Denial of Service:** - In a DOS attack, an attacker attempt to prevent legitimate users from accessing information or services. By targeting your computer and its network connection, network of sites you are tiring to use, an attacker may be able to prevent you from accessing emails, web sites, online accounts; other services that relay on the affected computer.

Information Assurance

Information Assurance assures that authorized users have access to authorized information at the authorized time. It does not matter whether the information is in storage, processing. The session provides an introduction to information Assurance as well as details that will help storage personal better understand its applicability in their own environments.

Measures that protect and defend information and information system by ensuring their availability, integrity, authentication, confidentialit

"Information Assurance defines and applies a collection of policies, standards, methodologies, services and mechanisms to maintain mission integrity with respect to people, process, technology, information and supporting infrastructure."

"Information Assurance provides for confidentiality, integrity, availability, utility, authenticity, no repudiation, authorized use and privacy of information in all forms."

Information Security Principles

Confidentiality

Confidentiality ensures that information can be access to only for authorized user.

Integrity

Integrity ensures that, information remains same in its original form.

Availability

Availability ensures that, information resource is ready for use within stated operational parameters.

Possession

Possession ensures that, resource remains in the custody of authorized personal.

Authenticity

Authenticity ensures that, information confirms to reality, it is not misrepresented as something it is not.

Privacy

Privacy ensures that, protection of personal information from observation or intrusion as well as adherence to relevant privacy compliances.

Questions

Q.1. What are the needs of Information Security. Explain it?

Q.2. What is information system threats/attacks and what are the types of information system threats?

Q.3. Write a short notes of the following:

    (*i*) Information security

    (*ii*) Passive and Active attacks

Q.4. Explain in details information security principles?

Chapter 3

CYBER SECURITY

"Cyber security" refers to the protection of everything that is potentially exposed to the Internet: our computers, smart phones and other devices; our personal data, information; our privacy.

The Internet is evolved as amazingly useful and versatile tool that has become indispensable for work, education, personal entertainment, and staying connected with family and friends. Use it responsibly, while taking care to protect yourself and your data, and you will continue to find it a valuable resource.

Cyber security also referred to as information technology security, focuses on protecting computers, networks, programs and data from unintended or unauthorized access, change or destruction.

Why is cyber security important?

Government, military, corporation financial institutions, hospitals and other business collect, process and store a great deal of confidential information on computers and transmit that data across networks to other computers. With the growing volume and sophistication of cyber attacks. Ongoing attention is required to protect sensitive business and personal information as well as safeguard national security.

Theft in cyber security

Technological and Psychological Trickery

A Primer on Identity Theft

Identity theft is considered the fastest-growing financial crime. It occurs when a thief assumes the victim's identity in order to apply for credit cards, loans or other benefits, in the victim's name, or uses this information to access your existing accounts. The thief will accumulate massive debt or deplete your current assets and then move on to another stolen identity.

The victim, meanwhile, may end up thousands of dollars in debt, with a ruined credit history or with an empty bank account. Until cleared up, this can make it difficult to find a job, buy a car or home, obtain a student loan, or engage in other activities that depend on the use of your own good name.

Phishing

Phishing in which criminals trick victims into handing over their personal information such as online passwords, Social Security or credit card numbers. It might be done by invading your computer with **spyware** that reads your personal information, or it may be as easy as stealing your wallet.

Malware

"Malware," or "malicious software," refers to programs designed to invade and disrupt victims' computers. Malware might be used to delete and destroy valuable information; slow the computer down to a standstill; or spy on and steal valuable personal data from the victim's computer.

1. Virus: The best-known types of malware are viruses and worms, which infect computers, replicate, and spread to other computers. They might be transmitted via email or across networks.

2. Trojan horse: Another type of malware is the Trojan horse. Like its namesake from Greek legend, a Trojan horse looks like a gift – but when you click on it, you're downloading a hidden enemy.

3. Spyware: Spyware is a type of malware that collects information without the victim's knowledge. Some forms of spyware gather personal information including login accounts and bank or credit card information. Some may redirect your browser to certain websites, send pop-up ads, and change your computer settings.

Phishing and Social Engineering

Through phishing and social engineering, computer hackers trick victims into handing over sensitive data – or downloading malware – without thinking twice.

Social engineering may take the form of emails or instant messages that appear to come from a trusted source. You may get fraudulent email that appears to come from your bank, a shopping website, a friend, or even the State government. The message may even contain links to a counterfeit version of the company's website, complete with genuine-looking graphics and corporate logos.

In a phishing attack, you may be asked to click on a link or fraudulent website which asks you to submit your personal data or account information – and end up giving it to an identity thief. Or you might receive a suspicious email with an attachment containing a virus. By opening the attachment, you may download a Trojan horse that gives complete access to your computer.

Cyber safety

Cyber-safety is a common term used to describe a set of practices, measures and/or actions you can take to protect personal information and your computer from attacks.

Security Measures in Cyber Safety

By implementing all seven of these security measures, you will protect yourself, others, and your computer from many common threats.

In most cases, implementing each of these security measures will only take a few minutes.

How to protect (Cyber security protection)

Install OS/Software Updates

- Updates-sometimes called patches-fix problems with your operating system (OS) (e.g., Windows XP, Windows Vista, Mac OS X) and software programs (e.g., Microsoft Office applications).

- Most new operating systems are set to download updates by default. After updates are downloaded, you will be asked to install them. Click yes!

- To download patches for your system and software, visit:

  - Windows Update: http://windowsupdate.microsoft.com to get or ensure you have all the latest operating system updates only. Newer Windows systems are set to download these updates by default.

  - Microsoft Update: http://www.update.microsoft.com/microsoftupdate/ to get or ensure you have all the latest OS **and** Microsoft Office software updates. You must sign up for this service.

  - Apple: http://www.apple.com/support

  - UNIX: Consult documentation or online help for system update information and instructions.

- Be sure to restart your computer after updates are installed so that the patches can be applied immediately.

Run Anti-Virus Software

- To avoid computer problems caused by viruses, install and run an anti-virus program like Sophos.

- Periodically, check to see if your anti-virus is up to date by opening your anti-virus program and checking the *Last updated:* date.

- Anti-virus software removes viruses, quarantines and repairs infected files, and can help prevent future viruses.

Prevent Identity Theft

- Don't give out financial account numbers, Social Security numbers, driver's license numbers or other personal identity information unless you know exactly who's receiving it. Protect others people's information as you would your own.

- Never send personal or confidential information via email or instant messages as these can be easily intercepted.

- Beware of phishing scams - a form of fraud that uses email messages that appear to be from a reputable business (often a financial institution) in an attempt to gain personal or account information. These often do not include a personal salutation. Never enter personal information into an online form you accessed via a link in an email you were not expecting. Legitimate businesses will not ask for personal information online.
- Order a copy of your credit report from each of the three major credit bureaus-Equifax, Experian, and Trans Union. Reports can be ordered online at each of the bureaus' Web sites. Make sure reports are accurate and include only those activities you have authorized.

Turn on Personal Firewalls

- Check your computer's security settings for a built-in personal firewall. If you have one, turn it on. Microsoft Vista and Mac OSX have built-in firewalls. For more information, see:
    - Mac Firewall

        (docs.info.apple.com/article.html?path=Mac/10.4/en/mh1042.html)

    - Microsoft Firewall (www.microsoft.com/windowsxp/using/networking/security/winfirewall.mspx)

    - Unix users should consult system documentation or online help for personal firewall instructions and/or recommendations.

- Once your firewall is turned on, test your firewall for open ports that could allow in viruses and hackers. Firewall scanners like the one on http://www.auditmypc.com/firewall-test.asp simplify this process.
- Firewalls act as protective barriers between computers and the internet.

Hackers search the Internet by sending out pings (calls) to random computers and wait for responses. Firewalls prevent your computer from responding to these calls.

Avoid Spyware/Adware

- Spyware and adware take up memory and can slow down your computer or cause other problems.
- Use Spybot and Ad-Aware to remove spyware/adware from your computer. UC Davis students, faculty and staff can get Spybot and Ad-Aware for free on the Internet Tools CD (available from IT Express in Shields Library).
- Watch for allusions to spyware and adware in user agreements before installing free software programs.
- Be wary of invitations to download software from unknown internet sources.

Protect Passwords

- Do not share your passwords, and always make new passwords difficult to guess by avoiding dictionary words, and mixing letters, numbers and punctuation.
- Do not use one of these common passwords or any variation of them: qwerty1, abc123, letmein, password1, iloveyou1, (yourname1), baseball1.
- Change your passwords periodically.
- When choosing a password:
  - Mix upper and lower case letters
  - Use a minimum of 8 characters
  - Use mnemonics to help you remember a difficult password
- Store passwords in a safe place. Consider using KeePass Password Safe (http://keepass.info/), Keychain (Mac) or an encrypted USB drive to store passwords. Avoid keeping passwords on a Post-it under your keyboard, on your monitor or in a drawer near your computer!

Back Up Important Files

- Reduce your risk of losing important files to a virus, computer crash, theft or disaster by creating back-up copies.
- Keep your critical files in one place on your computer's hard drive so you can easily create a back up copy.
- Save copies of your important documents and files to a CD, online back up service, flash or USB drive, or a server.
- Store your back-up media in a secure place away from your computer, in case of fire or theft.
- Test your back up media periodically to make sure the files are accessible and readable.

CYBER-SAFETY AT HOME

- Physically secure your computer by using security cables and locking doors and windows in the dorms and off-campus housing.
- Avoid leaving your laptop unsupervised and in plain view in the library or coffee house, or in your car, dorm room or home.
- Set up a user account and password to prevent unauthorized access to your computer files.

Do not install unnecessary programs on your computer.

CYBER-SAFETY AT WORK

- Be sure to work with your technical support coordinator before implementing new cyber-safety measures.

- Talk with your technical support coordinator about what cyber-safety measures are in place in your department.

- Report to your supervisor any cyber-safety policy violations, security flaws/weaknesses you discover or any suspicious activity by unauthorized individuals in your work area.

- Physically secure your computer by using security cables and locking building/office doors and windows.

Do not install unnecessary programs on your work computer.

The following tips are adapted from those offered by the United States Computer Emergency Readiness Team (US-CERT).

Virus Protection Tools

Use and maintain a reputable antivirus software. Good antivirus software packages recognize and protect your computer against most known viruses. (You can check online reviews to learn about the best versions currently available.) Once you have installed an antivirus package, you should use it to scan your entire computer periodically. Find a package that includes antispyware tools.

Keep antivirus software up to date. Install software patches and security updates for your antivirus software on a regular basis. They will help protect your computer against new threats as they are discovered. Many vendors and operating systems offer automatic updates.If this option is available, you should enable it.

Install or enable a firewall. Firewalls protect against outside attackers by shielding your computer or network from malicious or unnecessary Internet traffic. They are especially important for users who rely on "always on" connections such as cable or Digital Subscriber Line modems. Some operating systems include a firewall; if yours has one, you should make sure it is enabled. If not, consider purchasing a hardware- or software-based firewall.

Use antispyware tools. Many antivirus software packages are sold with antispyware tools included. *Note:* Many vendors produce antivirus software. Deciding which one to choose can be confusing. All antivirus software essentially perform the same function, so your decision may be driven by recommendations, particular features, availability or price.

It is not a good idea to install too many types of security software. Too many programs can affect the performance of your computer and the effectiveness of the software itself.

Check Your Web Browser's Privacy and Security Settings: Almost all computers and smart phones come already installed with one or more web browsers (such as Safari, Firefox, Internet Explorer, Chrome or others). The browsers come with default settings that seek to strike a balance between keeping your computer secure, and allowing you to get the functionality you expect from most websites.

Use Smart Passwords

Don't use passwords that are based on personal information a hacker can easily access or guess; and don't use words that can be found in the dictionary. One method for creating passwords is to rely on a series of words and memory techniques, or mnemonics, to help you remember how to decode it.

Don't Get Phished

Never trust an unsolicited email, text message, pop-up window, Facebook message, etc. that asks you to: give sensitive information such as your Social Security or bank account numbers; click on a link or open an attachment; or send someone money.

Don't trust the message no matter how convincing or official it looks; no matter if it appears to come from your bank, the government, your ISP, or your best friend.

Always independently verify the authenticity of the message before you respond. Don't use an email address, link, or phone number in the message itself. If it's from your bank, search online for the customer service line and call the bank.

Use common sense. Never open email attachments unless you know from whom they were sent. Never execute programs unless they are from a trusted source. Never click on links within pop-up windows. Be wary of free downloadable software, or any email link that offers antimalware programs.

Beware of homemade CDs, floppy disks and flash drives. If you plan to use them in your computer, scan them with your antivirus software first.

Questions

Q.1. What is cyber security and what are the needs of cyber security?

Q.2. Explain the list of primary theft in cyber security in details?

Q.3. Write a short notes of the following:

   (*i*) phising   (*ii*) viruses   (*iii*) trojon horse   (*iv*) malware   (*v*) spyware

Q.4. What is cyber safety and what are the security measures in cyber safety?

Chapter 4

INFORMATION SECURITY GOVERNANCE AND RISK MANAGEMENT

IT has become an integral part of everyday business and private life, though new technologies give unprecedented functionality it introduces new risks and environment harder to control. Increased dependency on IT means higher impact when things go wrong. A security breach will have a major impact. All are concerned about the privacy of their information and business losses and hence information security has become a part of IT Governance and corporate governance.

Information Security Governance

Information security governance is a subset of enterprise governance that provides strategic direction, ensures that objectives are achieved, manages risks appropriately, uses organisational resources responsibly, and monitors the success or failure of the enterprise security programme.

To achieve effective information security governance, management must establish and maintain a framework to guide the development and maintenance of a comprehensive information security programme. The information security governance framework generally consists of:

- An information security risk management methodology
- A comprehensive security strategy explicitly linked with business and IT objectives
- An effective security organisational structure
- A security strategy that talks about the value of information protected—and delivered
- Security policies that address each aspect of strategy, control and regulation
- A complete set of security standards for each policy to ensure that procedures and guidelines comply   with policy
- Institutionalised monitoring processes to ensure compliance and provide feedback on effectiveness and mitigation of risk
- A process to ensure continued evaluation and update of security policies, standards, procedures and risks

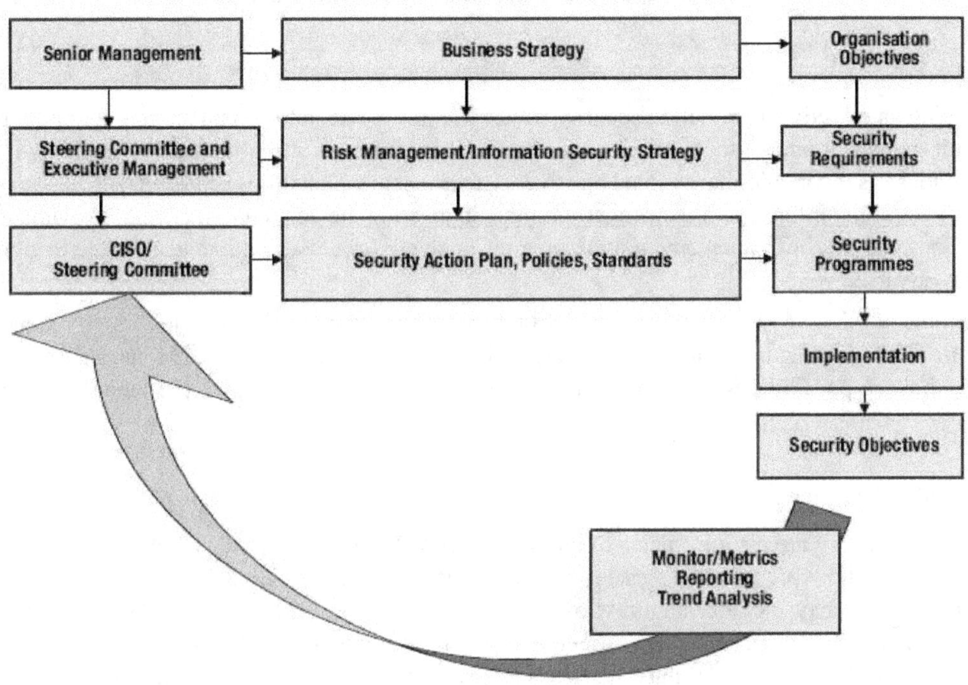

Fig. 4.1: Information security governance

Who should concerned with information security

Boards of Directors/Trustees

It is a fundamental responsibility of senior management to protect the interests of the organisation's stakeholders. This includes understanding risks to the business to ensure that they are adequately addressed from a governance perspective.

Information security governance requires strategic direction and impetus. It requires commitment, resources and assignment of responsibility for information security management, as well as a means for the board to determine that its intent has been met.

Members of the board need to be aware of the organisation's information assets and their criticality to ongoing business operations. This can be accomplished by periodically providing the board with the high-level results of comprehensive risk assessments and business impact analyses. It may also be accomplished by business dependency assessments of information resources. A result of these activities should include board members validating/ratifying the key assets they want protected and confirming that protection levels and priorities are appropriate to a recognised standard of due care.

Executives

Developing an effective information security strategy requires integration with and co-operation of business unit managers and process owners. A successful outcome is the alignment of information security activities in support of organisational bjectives. The extent to which this is achieved will determine the effectiveness of the information security programme in meeting the desired objective of providing a predictable, defined level of management assurance for business processes and an acceptable level of impact from adverse events.

An example of this is the foundation for the US federal government's cybersecurity, which requires assigning clear and unambiguous authority and responsibility for security, holding officials accountable for fulfilling those responsibilities, and integrating security requirements into budget and capital planning processes.

Steering Committee

Information security affects all aspects of an organisation. To ensure that all stakeholders affected by security considerations are involved, a steering committee of executives should be formed. Members of such a committee may include, amongst others, the chief executive officer (CEO) or designee, business unit executives, chief financial officer (CFO), chief information officer (CIO)/IT director, chief security officer (CSO), CISO, human resources, legal, risk management, audit, operations and public relations.

A steering committee serves as an effective communication channel for management's aims and directions and provides an ongoing basis for ensuring alignment of the security programme with organisational objectives. It is also instrumental in achieving behaviour change toward a culture that promotes good security practices and policy compliance.

Chief Information Security Officer

All organisations have a CISO whether or not anyone holds that title. It may be *de facto* the CIO, CSO, CFO or, in some cases, the CEO, even when there is an information security office or director in place. The scope and breadth of information security concerns are such that the authority required and the responsibility taken inevitably end up with a C-level officer or executive manager. Legal responsibility, by default, extends up the command structure and ultimately resides with senior management and the board of directors. Failure to recognise this and implement appropriate governance structures can result in senior management being unaware of this responsibility and the attendant liability. It usually results in a lack of effective alignment of security activities with organisational objectives.

Responsible for –

- determine priorities of security initiatives based on business needs
- defining the acceptable risk level for the organization
- developing security objectives and strategies
- reviewing risk assessment an dauditing reports
- monitoring the business impact of security risks
- reviewing major security breaches and incidents
- approving any major change to the security policy and program

Chief privacy officer

It reports to the chie security officer and responsible for –

- Ensuring that company. Customer and employee data are kept safe.
- Setting policy that how data are collected and protected.

Audit committee

Appointed by the board of directors and responsible for –

- The integrity of the company's financial statements and other financial information provided to stockholders and others
- The company's system of internal controls
- the engagement and performance of the independent auditors
- the performance of the internal audit function

Information owner

A business executive or business manager responsible for –

- Assigning initial information classification
- periodically reviewing the classification to ensure it meets business needs
- ensuring security controls are in place commensurate with the classification
- determining the security requirements, access criteria, and backup requirements for the information assets
- reviewing and ensuring currency of the access rights associated with the information assets

Information Custodian (Data Custodian)

An IT or operations person responsible for :

- Performing backups according to the backup requirements established by the Information Owner

- necessary, restoring lost of corrupted information backup media
- performing related management functions as required to ensure availability of the information to the business
- ensuring record retention requirements are met based on the Information Owner's analysis

System Owner

Personnel responsible for: integrating security considerations into application and system purchasing decisions and development projects ensuring that adequate security is being provided by the necessary controls, password management, remote access controls, operating system configurations, and so on ensuring the systems are properly assessed for vulnerabilities and must report any to the incident response team and Information Owners

Application Owner

Manager of the business unit who is accountable for performance of the business function served by the application, responsible for :

- establishing user access criteria and availability requirements of their applications
- ensuring the security controls associated with the application are commensurate with the highest level of information classification used by the application

User Manager (Supervisor)

The immediate manager or supervisor of an employee responsible for :-
- informing the Security Administrator of the transfer or termination of any employee
- reporting any security incident or suspected incident to Information Security
- ensuring the currency of user ID information such as employee ID and account information
- receiving and distributing initial passwords for newly created user IDs
- educating employees with regard to security policies, procedures, and standard for which they are accountable

Security Administrator

Any Company employee who owns and "administrative" User ID Responsible for :-
- understanding The different data environments and the impact of granting access to them
- ensuring Access requests are consistent with the policies and security guidelines
- administering Access rights according to criteria established by Information Owners
- creating And removing user IDs As directed by the User Manager

- administering the system security within the scope of their job description and functional responsibilities
- distributing and following up (with Information Owners) on security violation reports

Security Analyst

Strategic personnel responsible for:-

- developing Security policies, standards, and guidelines, as well as various baselines
- providing Data security design input, consulting, and review
- developing A basic understanding of the information to ensure proper controls are implemented

Change Control Analyst

Personnel Responsible for: analyzing The requested changes to the IT infrastructure, and determining the impact on applications, databases, data— related tools, etc.

Data Analyst

Personnel Responsible for: Designing Data structure to meet business needs designing Physical database structure creating And maintaining logical data models based on business requirements providing Technical assistance to Information Owners In developing data architectures recording Metadata in the data library creating, maintaining, and using metadata to effectively manage database deployment

Solution Provider

Aka integrator, application provider, programmer, IT Provider whose responsibilities are :

working With Data Analysts To ensure that the application and data will work together to meet business needs giving Technical requirements to Data Analysts To ensure performance and reporting requirements are met.

Process Owner

Personnel Responsible for the management, implementation, and continuous improvement of a process, by:

ensuring That data requirements are defined to support the business process (NOT Done by Information Owners).

working With Information Owners To define and champion data quality program for data within the process.

resolving data— related issues that span applications within business processes.

What should IS Security Governance deliver

Should provide strategic alignment, value delivery, risk management and performance measurement

1. Strategic alignment

- Security requirement driven by enterprise requirements
- Security solutions fit for enterprise processes
- Investment in information security aligned with enterprise strategy and agreed upon risk profile

2. Value delivery

- A standard set of security practices (baseline security following best practices)
- Properly prioritized and distributed effort to areas with great impact and business benefit
- Institutionalized and commoditised solutions
- Complete solutions covering organization and process as well as technology
- A continuous improvement culture

3. Risk Management

- Agreed upon risk profile
- Understanding of risk exposure
- Awareness of risk management priorities

4. Performance measurement

- Defined set of metrics
- Measurement process with feedback on progress made
- Independence assurance

Risks of Information Security

The following are some security risks –

- Physical damage (fire, water and natural disasters)
- Human error (accidental / intentional)
- Equipment mal functions (failure of systems and peripheral devices)
- Inside and outside attacks (hacking, cracking and other attacks)
- Misuse of data (sharing trade secrets, espionage, fraud and theft)
- Application error (computational errors, input errors, buffer overflows)

Risk

- The probability that a particular threat will exploit a particular vulnerability
- Need to systematically understand risks to a system and decide how to control them.

Risk analysis

Method of identifying risks, assessing the possible damage that could be caused to justify security safeguards. It is used to ensure that security is cost effective, relevant, timely and responsive to threats. Risk analysis helps to integrate security program objectives with company's business objectives and requirements. All these are required to be properly aligned for the success of the organization

or

The process of identifying, assessing, and reducing risks to an acceptable level:—

- Defines and controls threats and vulnerabilities
- Implements risk reduction measures

The process of analyzing a target environment and the relationships of its risk— related attributes

or

The process of measuring the likelihood of the undesirable event occuring of the event.

An analytic discipline with three parts:

- Risk assessment: determine what the risks are
- Risk management: evaluating alternatives for mitigating the risk
- Risk communication: presenting this material in an
- understandable way to decision makers and/or the public

Risk analysis and risk management serve as tools to develop and maintain a covered entity's strategy to protect the confidentiality, integrity

Risk Analysis Terminology

In order to discuss security risk analysis concepts we must first establish a baseline of the related terms. Then, we must define how the terms relate to each other and how they are used to analyze risk.

Asset - Anything with value and in need of protection.

Threat - An action or potential action with the propensity to cause damage.

Vulnerability - A condition of weakness. If there were no vulnerabilities, there would be no concern for threat activity.

RISK - A Vulnerability triggered or exploited by a Threat equals a Risk.

Countermeasure - Any device or action with the ability to reduce vulnerability.

Expected Loss - The anticipated negative impact to assets due to threat manifestation.

Impact - Losses as a result of threat activity are normally expressed in one or more impact areas. Four areas are commonly used; Destruction, Denial of Service, Disclosure, and Modification.

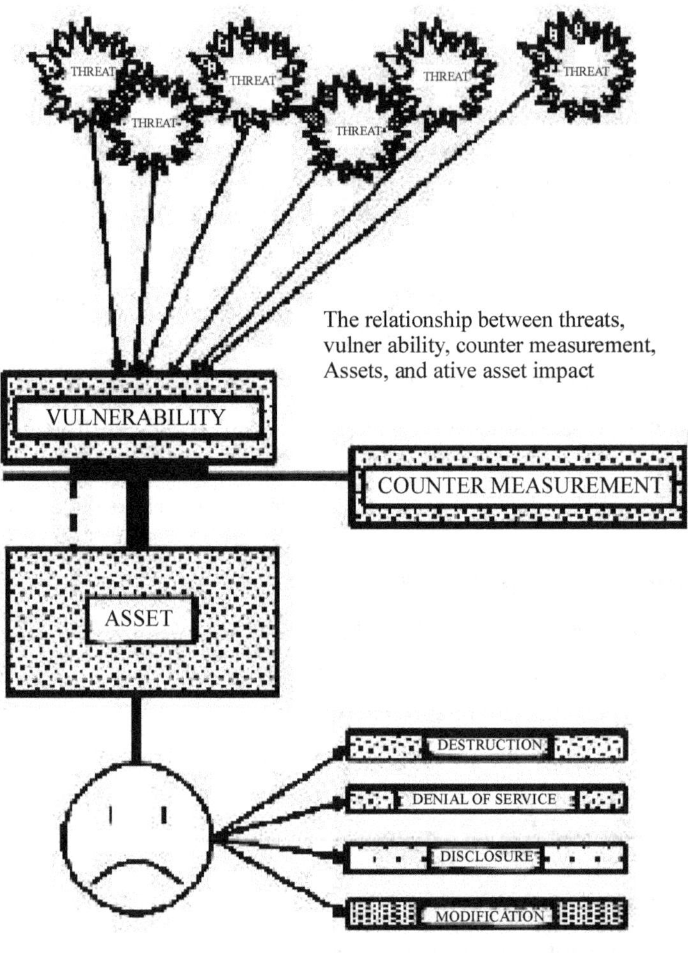

Fig. 4.2

A security risk analysis is an examination of the interrelationships between assets, threats, vulnerabilities, and countermeasures to determine the **current** level of risk. The level of risk that remains after consideration of all in-place countermeasures, vulnerability levels, and related threats is called **residual risk.** Ultimately, it is the residual risk that must be accepted [as is] or reduced to a point where it can be accepted.

The relationship between the elements of a risk analysis is illustrated in the graph at above. Any given threat in the population of threats is poised to take advantage of system vulnerabilities, countermeasures reduce the level of vulnerability, the asset is what needs to be protected, and the impacts are the result of threat activity through residual risk.

Benefits of Risk Analysis

- Assurance that greatest risks have bee identified and addressed
- Increased understanding of risks
- Mechanism for reaching consensus
- Support for needed controls
- Means for communicating results

Risk Analysis and Risk Management Steps

There are numerous methods of performing risk analysis and risk management. There is no single method or "best practice" that guarantees compliance with the Security Rule. However, most risk analysis and risk management processes have common steps. The following steps are provided as examples of steps covered entities could apply to their environment. The steps are adapted from the approach outlined in NIST SP 800-30.

RISK ANALYSIS STEPS:

1. Assign value to asset.

- What is its value in the company?
- How much did it cost to acquire or develop?
- How much does it cost to maintain?
- How much does it make in profits for the company?
- How much would it be worth to the competition?
- How much would it cost to re— create or recover?
- Estimate potential loss per

2. Estimate potential loss per threat

Some of the questionsare:

- How much would the damage cost?
- What is the value lost if critical devices fail or confidential information is disclosed.
- What is the cost of recovering from the threat ?
- What is the single loss expectancy for each asset corrosponding to each threat ?

3. Perform a threat analysis

Gather information about the likelihood of each threat by examining past record and official security resources that provide the kind of data.

4. Derived the overall annualized loss potential per threat.

- Combined potential loss and probability.
- Calculate the **annualized loss expectancy** per threat, using info from the past three steps
- Choose remedial measures to counteract each threat

5. Mitigate, transfer, avoid, or accept the risk

Questions

Q.1. Explain in details of Information Security Governance?

Q.2. Who should concern with information security?

Q.3. Write a short notes of the following:

(*i*) Security Administrator　　(*ii*) Security analyst　　(*iii*) Data Analysis

(*iv*) Risk Management

Q.4. Explain in details Risk analysis and give the advantages of risk analysis?

Q.5. Explain in details Risk Analysis Terminology?

Q.7. What are the steps of risk analysis?

Chapter 5

APPLICATION SECURITY AND DATA SECURITY CONSIDERATION

Application Security

Most security professionals understand the importance of finding and eliminating application vulnerabilities. Exploitation of Internet-exposed applications is the leading threat to critical business data and sensitive customer information. Further, recent studies show that the major barrier to effective application security programs is the lack of management buy-in for required resources.

Definition of Application Security

There are a number of definitions for application security.

In broad terms**, "Application security is about understanding, assessing and managing the risks to an organization's application portfolio".**

The Critical Security Controls (CSCs) effort **defines "Application Software Security as the processes and tools organizations use to detect/prevent/correct security weaknesses in the development and acquisition of software applications."**

Critical Security Controls documentation expands this definition to include mitigating application-level vulnerabilities during the deployment and operation of applications. This captures the basic goal of any application security program: reducing application vulnerabilities before they are deployed and reducing the likelihood of successful exploitation of any vulnerability that does make it into production.

Why do we need Application Security

Web applications have become the prime targets for several reasons:

1. By definition, web-based applications are exposed to the Internet with standard interfaces. Attackers can easily discover applications and look for vulnerabilities.

2. Common wisdom dictates that websites need to be refreshed constantly in order to attract and retain users. This often leads to shortcutting configuration management and control procedures, resulting in untested and misconfigured web applications being exposed.

3. Web applications generally consist of hybrids of off-the-shelf software, business- or contractor developed applications and open source components. Much of the vulnerability in these components goes unnoticed until exploited or a patch notification arrives. In addition, the volatility and complexity of these components can render software development and testing processes ineffective.

Web applications provide attackers with a good launching point to penetrate into the organization, such as a connected database, or to exploit the site in order to download malware onto the computer of customers visiting the site.

Understanding Secure Life Cycle Practices

An application security program needs to span the full life cycle of applications.

This includes the design and development phase; through coding, integration and testing; into final certification accreditation testing prior to production release; with ongoing vulnerability monitoring and shielding for production applications. Security reviews should be part of all of those phases, using manual processes where necessary, but taking advantage of technology where possible. From a process, controls and technology point of view, this includes:

- **Static application testing:** Detecting and correcting vulnerabilities in individual components of an application at the source, at object code or at binary level.

- **Dynamic application testing:** Detecting vulnerabilities using penetration-testing techniques at the "black box" level during final QA and during operational use.

- **Application-level vulnerability shielding:** Deploying and managing technologies such as application level or web application firewalls, to prevent the exploitation of vulnerabilities in operational applications before patches or updates can be applied.

Data Security Consideration

Backing up your data is an essential security measure in today's computing environment. Data has gained intrinsic value, either in the manpower needed to generate that data or in the significance of that data to your customers.

Data loss, both accidental and due to theft, costs hundreds of millions of dollars every year. When taken as a whole one thing becomes clear, your data must be protected.

Terminologies of Data Security Consideration:

• **Data Protection:** It includes topics such as backups, archives, and preservation, physical security and encryption.

Terms "backups" and "archives" are often used interchangeably, but do have different meanings:

- Backups: a copy (or copies) of the original file is made before the original is over written means if my data is lost than we can gain again the data or file.
- Archives: preservation of the file means any file have some importance in any file or system.
- **Data Preservation:** It includes archiving in addition to processes such as data rescue, data reformatting, data conversion, metadata.

Difference between backup and archiving:

• Backups

- Used to take periodic snapshots of data in case the current version is destroyed or lost
- Backups are copies of files stored for short or near-long-term
- Often performed on a somewhat frequent schedule

• Archiving

- Used to preserve data for historical reference or potentially during disasters
- Archives are usually the final version, stored for long-term, and generally not copied over
- Often performed at the end of a project or during major milestones

Note: It is a good method to have multiple copies of your backups and one copy of your archive.

Needs of Data Backup

- By the help of Data Backup we can save time, money, productivity.
- By the help of Data Backup we can Reproduce results of past procedures (if they were based on older files)
- Limit liability
- By the help of Data Backup we can prepare for disasters
  - Accidental deletions
  - Fires, natural disasters
  - Software bugs, hardware failures

Considerations

Consideration means we should do backup our data or file in the system and It have many queries which of the following:

How often should you do backups?

What kind of backups should you perform?

What about non-digital files?

Where will you backup your files?

How are backups carried out?

What do I do if I need to get a file off of backups?

How do you verify a backup has been successfully performed?

How do you verify a backup has been successfully performed?

Are there backups of the backups?

How long do you keep your backups?

What happens to the backups after the project is no longer funded, project ends, or staff departs?

• Data Conversions and Formats

- Use non-proprietary, standard formats
- Convert text files from .doc or .xls to .txt, image files to .tiff or .pdf
- Be sure to check files after converting them, as data, metadata, and formatting loss can occur

• Versioning

- Use consecutive numbers and letters to help keep track of changes to a file throughout various edits and revisions. This will help you quickly differentiate between files with similar names.

• File Naming

- Use file names that are consistent, descriptive, and concise so that you can find and quickly identify the file the file at a later time.
- Rename files that have a default file name when exported such as "image.jpg" or "archive.zip"

Questions

Q.1. Define Application Security and what are the needs of Application Security?

Q.2. Explain in details data security consideration?

Q.3. Write a short notes of the following:

    (*i*)   Data Protection

    (*ii*) Data Preservation

Q.4. What are the difference between backup and archiving?

Q.5. What are the needs of data backup?

Chapter 6

SECURITY TECHNOLOGIES

Firewall

A firewall is an integrated collection of security measures designed to prevent unauthorized electronic access to a networked computer system.

"A network firewall is similar to firewalls in building construction, because in both cases they are intended to isolate one "network" or "compartment" from another."

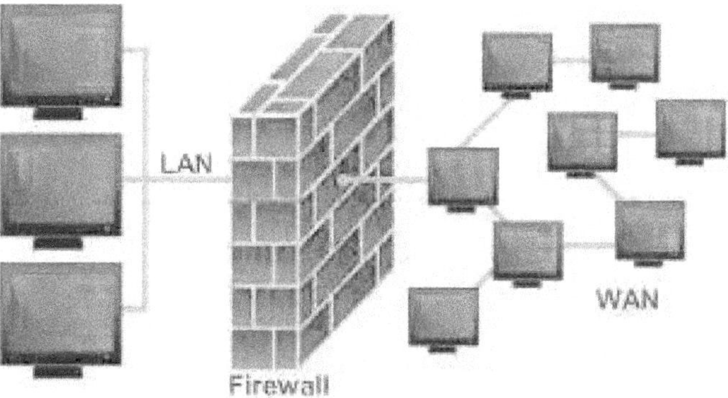

Fig. 6.1

Types of Firewall

1. Packet filters (stateless)

- If a packet matches the packet filter's set of rules, the packet filter will drop or accept it.

The most basic type of firewall is a packet filter. It receives packets and evaluates them according to a set of rules that are usually in the form of access control lists. These packets may be forwarded to their destinations, dropped, or dropped with a return message to the originator describing what happened. The types of filtering rules vary from one vendor's product to another, but those most frequently applied are:

- Source and destination IP address (e.g., all packets from source address 128.44.9.0 through 128.44.9.255 might be accepted, but all other packets might be rejected).

- Source and destination port (e.g., all TCP packets originating from or destined to port 25—the simple mail transfer protocol, or SMTP, port— might be accepted, but all TCP packets destined for port 79—the finger port—might be dropped).

- Direction of traffic (e.g., inbound or outbound).

- Type of protocol (e.g., IP, TCP, user datagram protocol, or internetwork packet exchange).

- The packet's state (i.e., SYN, meaning synchronize, or ACK, which is the acknowledgement that a connection between hosts has already been established).

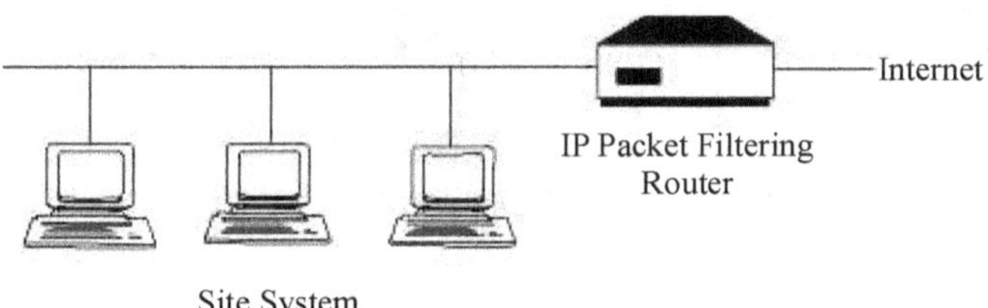

Fig. 6.2

Stateful filter

- it maintains records of all connections passing through it and can determine if a packet is either the start of a new connection, a part of an existing connection, or is an invalid packet.

Application layer

- It works like a proxy it can "understand" certain applications and protocols.

- It may inspect the contents of the traffic, blocking what it views as inappropriate content (i.e. websites, viruses, vulnerabilities, ...)

Stateless Firewalls

- A stateless firewall doesn't maintain any remembered context (or "state") with respect to the packets it is processing. Instead, it treats each packet attempting to travel through it in isolation without considering packets that it has processed previously.

Statefull Firewalls

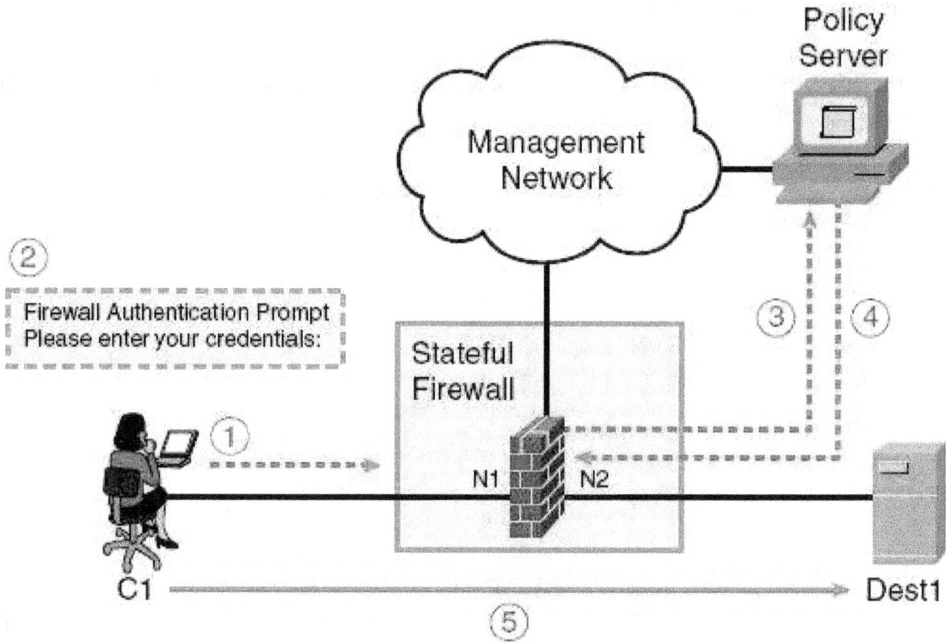

Fig. 6.3: Stateful Firewalls and Identity Awareness

- Stateful firewalls can tell when packets are part of legitimate sessions originating within a trusted network.

- Stateful firewalls maintain tables containing information on each active connection, including the IP addresses, ports, and sequence numbers of packets.

- Using these tables, stateful firewalls can allow only inbound TCP packets that are in response to a connection initiated from within the internal network.

VPN (Virtual Private Network)

Virtual

Virtual means not real or in a different state of being. In a VPN, private communication between two or more devices is achieved through a public network the Internet. Therefore, the communication is virtually but not physically there.

Private

Private means to keep something a secret from the general public. Although those two devices are communicating with each other in a public environment, there is no third party who can interrupt this communication or receive any data that is exchanged between them.

Network

A network consists of two or more devices that can freely and electronically communicate with each other via cables and wire. A VPN is a network. It can transmit information over long distances effectively and efficiently.

The term VPN has been associated in the past with such remote connectivity services as the (PSTN), Public Switched Telephone Network but VPN networks have finally started to be linked with IP-based data networking.

Before IP based networking corporations had expended considerable amounts of time and resources, to set up complex private networks, now commonly called Intranets.

These networks were installed using costly leased line services, Frame Relay, and ATM to incorporate remote users. For the smaller sites and mobile workers on the remote end, companies supplemented their networks with remote access servers or ISDN.

Small to medium-sized companies, who could not afford dedicated leased lines, used low-speed switched services.

Today's VPN solutions overcome the security factor using special tunneling protocols and complex encryption procedures, data integrity and privacy is achieved, and the new connection produces what seems to be a dedicated point-to point connection.

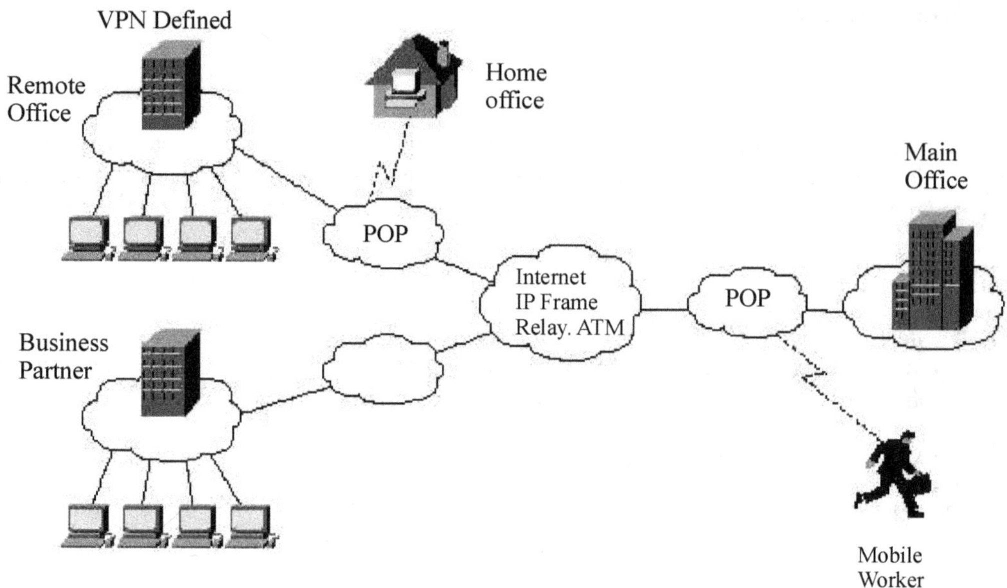

Fig. 6.4

Categories of VPN

1. **Trusted VPN:** A customer "trusted" the leased circuits of a service provider and used it to communicate without interruption. Although it is "trusted" it is not secured.

2. **Secure VPN:** With security becoming more of an issue for users, encryption and decryption was used on both ends to safeguard the information passed to and fro. This ensured the security needed to satisfy corporations, customers, and providers.

3. **Hybrid VPN:** A mix of a secure and trusted VPN. A customer controls the secure parts of the VPN while the provider, such as an ISP, guarantees the trusted aspect.

4. **Provider-provisioned VPN:** A VPN that is administered by a service provider.

Types of VPN

Remote access VPNs

Remote access VPN enables mobile users to establish a connection to an organization server by using the infrastructure provided by an ISP (Internet Services Provider). Remote access VPN allows users to connect to their corporate intranets or extranets wherever or whenever is needed. Users have access to all the resources on the organization's network as if they are physically located in organization.

The user connects to a local ISP that supports VPN using plain old telephone services (POTS), integrated services digital network (ISDN), digital subscriber line (DSL), etc. The VPN device at the ISP accepts the user's login, then establishes the tunnel to the VPN device at the organization's office and finally begins forwarding packets over the Internet. Remote access VPN offers advantages such as:

- Reduced capital costs associated with modem and terminal server equipment

- Greater scalability and easy to add new users

- Reduced long-distance telecommunications costs, nationwide toll-free 800 number is no longer needed to connect to the organization's modems

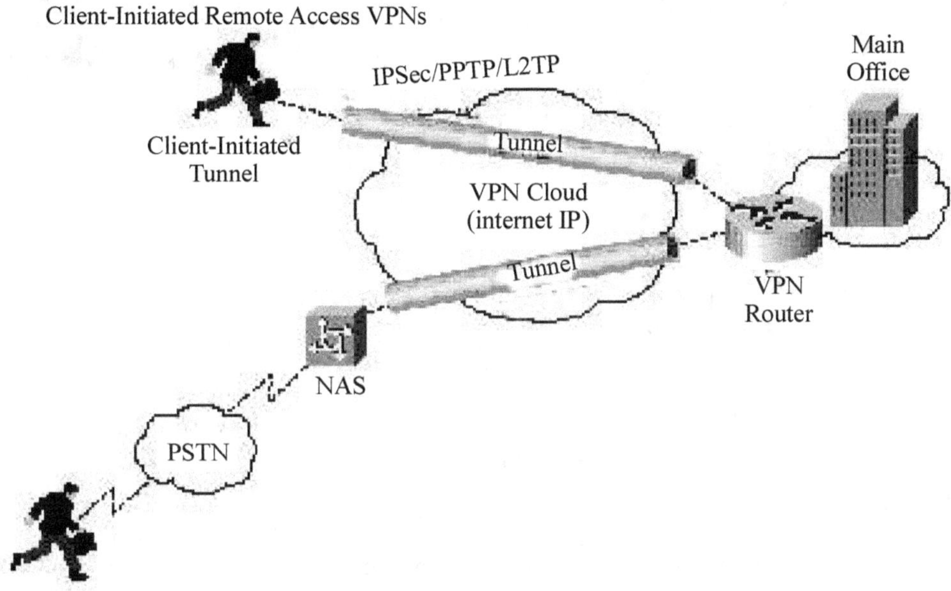

Fig. 6.5

Intranet VPNs

Intranet VPN provides virtual circuits between organization offices over the Internet   They are built using the Internet, service provider IP, Frame Relay, or ATM networks. An IP WAN infrastructure uses IPSec or GRE to create secure traffic tunnels across the network. Benefits of an intranet VPN include the following:

- Reduced WAN bandwidth costs, efficient use of WAN bandwidth

- Flexible topologies

- Congestion avoidance with the use of bandwidth management traffic shaping

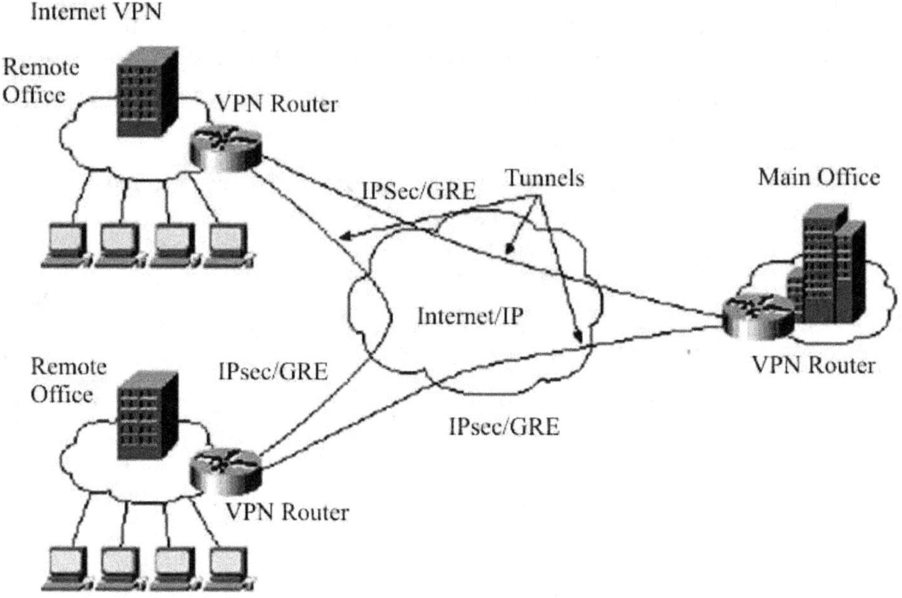

Fig. 6.6

Extranet VPNs

The concept of setting up extranet VPN is the same as intranet VPN. The only difference is the users. Extranet VPN are built for users such as customers, suppliers, or different organizations over the Internet.

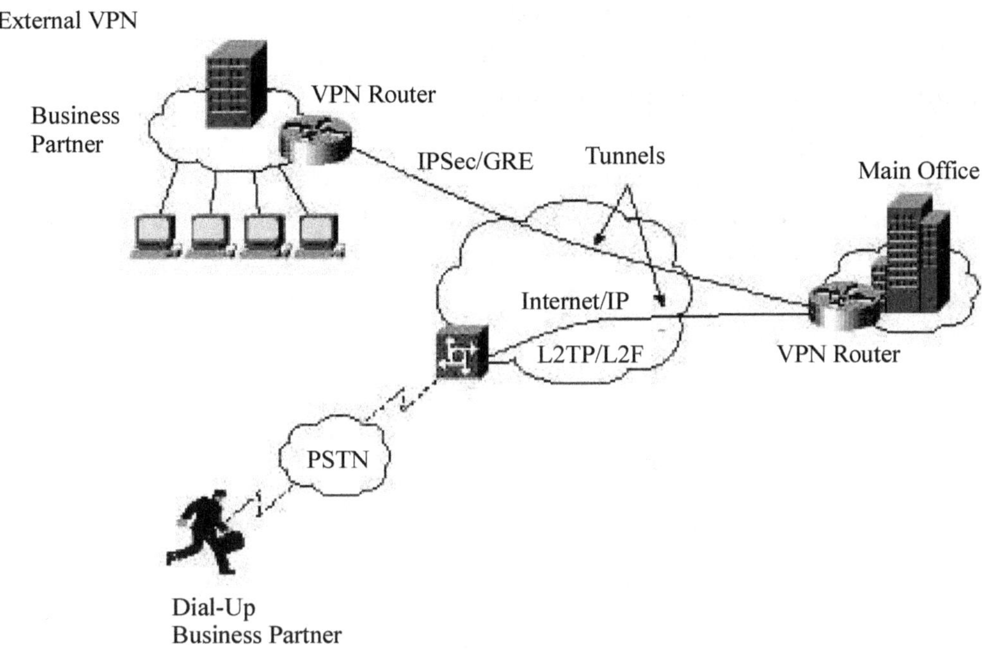

Fig. 6.7

Advantages of VPNs

- **Extends Geographic Connectivity-**

  A VPN connects remote workers to central resources, making it easier to set up global operations.

- **Boosts Employee Productivity-**

  A VPN solution enables telecommuters to boost their productivity by eliminating time-consuming commutes and by creating uninterrupted time for focused work.

- **Improves Internet Security –**

  An always on broadband connection to the Internet makes a network vulnerable to hacker attacks. Many VPN solutions include additional security measures, such as firewalls and anti-virus checks to counteract the different types of network security threats.

- **Scales Easily –**

  A VPN allows companies to utilize the remote access infrastructure within ISPs. Therefore, companies are able to add a virtually unlimited amount of capacity without adding significant infrastructure.

Questions

Q.1. Explain any one security technology in details?

Q.2. What is firewall and what are the types of firewall?

Q.3. Define VPN and what are the types of virtual private network?

Q.4. What are the advantages of VPN?

Q.5. What are the categories of virtual private network, explain it?

Q.6. Explain the main methods or technologies used for data secured? Explain also vulnerabilities with Virtual Private Networks?

Chapter 7

SECURITY THREATS

Whenever an individual or an organization creates a web site or has a web presence, they are vulnerable to security attacks. Security attacks are mainly aimed at stealing, altering or destroying personal and confidential information, stealing the hard drive space, illegally accessing passwords to get to the private account information from the online banking services.

Types of security threats

Hacker attacks

Hacking, by definition is to use a computer to break into the security of a remote computer. Hacker attacks can be identified as under of the following:

Viruses or Worm

Computer virus is a computer program that can copy itself and infect a computer without permission or knowledge of the user. The original may modify the copies or the copies may modify themselves, as occurs in a metamorphic virus. A virus can only spread from one computer to another when its host is taken to the uninfected computer, for instance by a user sending it over a network or carrying it on a removable medium such as a floppy disk CD, or USB drive.

Viruses can spread to other computers by infecting files on a network file system or a file system that is accessed by another computer. Many personal computers are now connected to the Internet and to local-area networks, facilitating their spread. Today's viruses may also take advantage of network services such as the World Wide Web and file sharing systems to spread, blurring the line between viruses and worms. Furthermore, some sources use an alternative terminology in which a virus is any form of self-replicating malware.

A computer virus reproduces by making, possibly modified, copies of itself in the computer's memory, storage, or over a network. This is similar to the way a biological virus works.

A computer virus or a computer worm is a malicious software program that can self-replicate on computers or via computer networks – without you being aware that your machine has become infected. Because each subsequent copy of the virus or computer worm can also self-replicate, infections can spread very rapidly. There are very many different types of computer viruses and computer worms – and many can cause high levels of destruction.

Classification of virus

Viruses can be subdivided into a number of types based on their features.

Macro viruses

A macro virus, often written in the scripting languages for programs such as Word and Excel, is spread by infecting documents and spreadsheets. Since macro viruses are written in the language of the application and not in that of the operating system, they are known to be platform independent. They can spread between Windows, Mac and any other system, so long as they are running the required application. With the ever-increasing capabilities of macro languages in applications, and the possibility of infections spreading over networks, these viruses are major threats.

Network viruses

This kind of virus is proficient in quickly spreading across a Local Area Network (LAN) or even over the Internet. Usually, it propagates through shared resources, such as shared drives and folders. Once it infects a new system, it searches for potential targets by searching the network for other vulnerable systems. Once a new vulnerable system is found, the network virus infects the other system, and thus spreads over the network. Some of the most notorious network viruses are Nimda and SQLSlammer.

Companion virus

A companion virus does not have host files per se, but exploits MS-DOS. A companion virus creates new files (typically .COM but can also use other extensions such as ".EXD") that have the same file names as legitimate .EXE files. When a user types in the name of a desired program, if a user does not type in ".EXE" but instead does not specify a file extension, DOS will assume he meant the file with the extension that comes first in alphabetical order and run the virus. For instance, if a user had "(filename).COM" (the virus) and "(filename).EXE" and the user typed "filename", he will run "(filename).COM" and run the virus. The virus will spread and do other tasks before redirecting to the legitimate file, which operates normally.

Spoofing

Spoofing is a scenario in which one person or program disguises as another by fabricating information and thereby gaining an illegal entry into the victim's confidential data. Spoofing comes in various flavors.

Web page spoofing- In this attack, a legitimate web page such as a bank's site is recreated in to look like the original one which is under control of the attacker. This is also called as "phishing". The idea is to mislead the users into thinking that they are connected to a trusted web site, and "steal" passwords and other private data. Once the users enter their password, the attack-code generates an error, and then redirects the user back to the legitimate site.

Email spoofing- It occurs when a user receives email that appears to have originated from one source when it actually was sent from another source. It is an attempt to trick the user into releasing sensitive information (such as passwords).

Phishing

Phishing occurs when an individual pretends to be a familiar organization or institution

- The phisher sends e-mail messages to people asking them to click a link to update or "confirm" personal information
- This information is stolen by the phisher
- phishers use spoofed sites to make their victims believe that they are visiting the organization's real Web site

Trojan Horse

A Trojan Horse is a malicious application that is designed to enable hackers to remotely access the target computer system. A Trojan Horse neither replicates nor copies itself, it must be sent by someone or carried by another program and may arrive in the form of a software of some sort. Trojans may arrive via unwanted downloads on compromised websites or install via online games or other internet-driven applications.

Trojans are malicious programs that perform actions that have not been authorized by the user. These actions can include:-

- Deleting data
- Blocking data
- Modifying data
- Copying data

Disrupting the performance of computers or computer networks

Unlike computer viruses and worms, Trojans are not able to self-replicate.

How Trojans can impact you

Trojans are classified according to the type of actions that they can perform on your computer:

Backdoor

A backdoor Trojan gives malicious users remote control over the infected computer. They enable the author to do anything they wish on the infected computer – including sending, receiving, launching and deleting files, displaying data and rebooting the computer. Backdoor Trojans are often used to unite a group of victim computers to form a botnet or zombie network that can be used for criminal purposes.

Exploit

Exploits are programs that contain data or code that takes advantage of vulnerability within application software that's running on your computer.

Rootkit

Rootkits are designed to conceal certain objects or activities in your system. Often their main purpose is to prevent malicious programs being detected – in order to extend the period in which programs can run on an infected computer.

Trojan-Banker

Trojan-Banker programs are designed to steal your account data for online banking systems,   e-payment systems and credit or debit cards.

Trojan-DDoS

These programs conduct DoS (Denial of Service) attacks against a targeted web address. By sending multiple requests – from your computer and several other infected computers – the attack can overwhelm the target address… leading to a denial of service.

Trojan-Downloader

Trojan-Downloaders can download and install new versions of malicious programs onto your computer – including Trojans and adware.

Trojan-Dropper

These programs are used by hackers in order to install Trojans and / or viruses – or to prevent the detection of malicious programs. Not all antivirus programs are capable of scanning all of the components inside this type of Trojan.

Trojan-FakeAV

Trojan-FakeAV programs simulate the activity of antivirus software. They are designed to extort money from you – in return for the detection and removal of threats… even though the threats that they report are actually non-existent.

Trojan-GameThief

This type of program steals user account information from online gamers.

Trojan-IM

Trojan-IM programs steal your logins and passwords for instant messaging programs – such as ICQ, MSN Messenger, AOL Instant Messenger, Yahoo Pager, Skype and many more.

Trojan-Ransom

This type of Trojan can modify data on your computer – so that your computer doesn't run correctly or you can no longer use specific data. The criminal will only restore your computer's performance or unblock your data, after you have paid them the ransom money that they demand.

Trojan-SMS

These programs can cost you money – by sending text messages from your mobile device to premium rate phone numbers.

Bomb or Logic bomb

In a computer program, a logic bomb, also called slag code, is programming code, inserted surreptitiously or intentionally, that is designed to execute (or "explode") under circumstances such as the lapse of a certain amount of time or the failure of a a program user to respond to a program command.

or

Logic bombs are small programs or sections of a program triggered by some event such as a certain date or time, a certain percentage of disk space filled, the removal of a file, and so on. For example, a programmer could establish a logic bomb to delete critical sections of code if she is terminated from the company. Logic bombs are most commonly installed by insiders with access to the system.

Trap doors

Trap doors, also referred to as backdoors, are bits of code embedded in programs by the programmer(s) to quickly gain access at a later time, often during the testing or debugging phase. If an unscrupulous programmer purposely leaves this code in or simply forgets to remove it, a potential security hole is introduced. Hackers often plant a backdoor on previously compromised systems to gain later access. Trap doors can be almost impossible to remove in a reliable manner. Often, reformatting the system is the only sure way.

Email Viruses

An e-mail virus is computer code sent to you as an e-mail note attachment which, if activated, will cause some unexpected and usually harmful effect, such as destroying certain files on your hard disk and causing the attachment to be remailed to everyone in your address book.

Malware

Malware short for "Malicious" software is designed to infiltrate or damage a computer system without the owner's informed consent.

Malware fundamentally disregards a user's choice regarding how his or her computer will be used.

Malicious software can be divided into different categories which includes viruses, worms, Trojans, and spyware.

Malware has the ability to hijack your web browser, redirect your search engine, bombard your screen with pop-ups and monitor your activity.

Spyware

Spyware is tracking software that hides itself (runs in the background) and gathers information without the computer owner's or user's knowledge or permission for the benefit of someone else.

Spyware can compromise the safety of your passwords, logon information, financial, or personal information.

Other spyware will record your actions and browsing habits on the internet. Any information collected by spyware is usually with the intent to sell.

What spyware and malware have in common is the ability to collect and distribute your personal information without your permission.

Adware

Adware is another form of malware and is exactly as the name suggests, software with advertising.

Adware can be downloaded and sometimes included in free programs. For example Windows Live messenger and Yahoo messenger contain adware.

Although some programs give the option not to install the extra adware, others seem to sneak it in without permission.

Questions

Q.1. Define Security Threats and what are the types of security threats?

Q.2. Explain in details about virus and classify virus ?

Q.3. Write a short notes of the following:

   (i) Phising   *(ii)* Viruses   *(iii)* Trojon horse   (iv) Malware

   (v) Spyware   *(vi)* E-mail Virus *(vii)* Adware   (viii) Trap doors

  (ix) Bomb or Logic bomb   *(x)* Trojan-SMS

Chapter 8

NETWORK SECURITY

Network Security is the protection of networking compoenent, connection and contents.

Types of network attacks

Reconnaissance attack is a kind of information gathering on network system and services. This enables the attacker to discover vulnerabilities or weaknesses on the network. It could be likened to a thief surveying through a car parking lot for vulnerable – unlocked - cars to break into and steal Reconnaissance attacks can consist of:

(*a*) Internet information lookup

(*b*) Ping sweeps

(*c*) Port scans

(*d*) Packet sniffers

Network intruders can use Internet tools, such as the nslookup and whois utilities, to easily determine the IP address space assigned to a given organisation or network. After finding out the IP address, the intruder can then ping the publicly available IP addresses to identify the addresses that are active.

There are automate ping sweep tool which an attacker can use, such as fping or gping, these tools methodically pings all network addresses in a given range or subnet. This is like to going through a section of a telephone directory and calling each number to know who answers.

When the attacker discovers active IP addresses, the intruder or attacker uses a port scanner (Nmap or Superscan -softwares designed to search a network host for open ports) to determine which network services or ports are active on the active IP addresses. The port scanner queries the ports to determine the application or operating system (OS) type and version, running on the targeted host. Based on the information gathered, the intruder can determine if a possible vulnerability or weakness that can be exploited exists.

Packet sniffing or Network snooping are common terms for eavesdropping. The information gathered by eavesdropping can be used to pose other attacks to the network.

A common method for eavesdropping on communications on a network is to capture TCP/IP or other protocol packets and decode the contents using a protocol analyzer or similar tools such as wire shark. After packets are captured, they can be examined for vulnerable information.

An intruder to eavesdrop on a management protocol called SNMP can use protocol analyser or wire shark.

SNMP provides a means for network devices to collect information about their status and to send it to an administrator. An intruder could eavesdrop on SNMP versin1 queries and gather valuable information on network devices configuration.

Network Access Attacks

Technology is forever evolving, so is hacking. It might come as a surprise to many that, as one wakes up in the morning and prepares for work, gets to the office and spends nine to twelve hour working; the same way a professional hacker spends all day modifying hacking techniques and looking for networks to exploit.

Firstly, for an attacker to gain access to a system network, the intruder has to find out the vulnerabilities or weaknesses in the network authentication, FTP and web services. Finding and exploiting these vulnerabilities will enable the attacker to gain access to web account and other confidential or sensitive information.

Types of access attacks

1. Password attack
2. Trust Exploitation
3. Port Redirection
4. Man-in-the middle attack

Password Attacks

A Network attacker uses packet sniffer tools to obtain user accounts and passwords information. Normally we log in and out of a system using authentication passwords to shared resources in a router or server, an attacker also repeatedly attempts to log in to a shared resource or to gain unauthorized access to an organization's network; this can also be referred to as dictionary or brute force attacks. To carry out this type of attacks, the intruder can use tools like the L0phtCrackor Cain.

These software or programs repeatedly attempt to log in as a user using words derived from a dictionary. Most dictionary attacks often succeed because network users often choose simple and short passwords, single words that are easy to predict.

Another password attack method uses what is called rainbow tables. A rainbow table is precompiled series of passwords, which is constructed by building chains of possible plain text passwords. Each chain is developed by starting with a randomly selected "guess" of the plain text password then sequentially applies variations on it. The attack software will apply the passwords in the rainbow table until it at a possible password. To conduct a rainbow table attack, attackers can use a tool such as L0phtCrack.

A brute-force attack tool is more sophisticated because it searches in detail using combinations of character sets to work out every possible password made up of those characters. The only disadvantage is that it takes much time to complete this type of attack. Brute-force attack tools have been known to solve simple passwords in less than a minute. Longer, more complex passwords may take days or weeks to resolve.

Solution of Password attack

1. Educating users to use complex password.
2. Restricting the number of failed login attempts.

Trust Exploitations Attack

The goal of a trust exploitation attacker is to compromise a trusted host, using it to stage attacks on other hosts in a network. If a host in a network of a company is protected by a firewall (inside host), but is accessible to a trusted host outside the firewall (outside host), the inside host can be attacked through the trusted outside host.

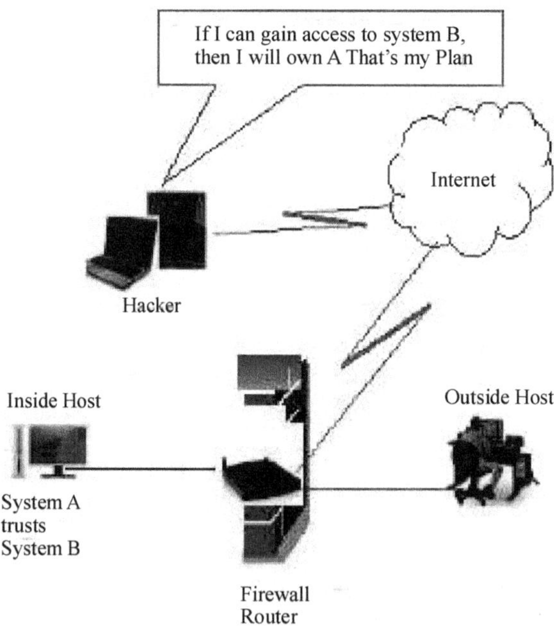

Fig. 8.1

Solution of Trust Exploitations Attack

Trust exploitation-based attacks can be controlled through strict protocols on trust levels within a network, for example, private VLANs can be deployed in public-service segments where multiple public servers are available.

Systems on the outside of a firewall should never be totally trusted by systems on the inside of a firewall. Such trust should be limited to specific protocols and should be authenticated by something other than an IP address.

Port Redirection Attack

A port redirection attack is another type of attack based on trust exploitation. The attacker uses a compromised host to gain access through a firewall that would otherwise be blocked.

Look at it this way; the host on the outside can get to the host on the public services segment, but not the host on the inside. If an intruder is able to compromise the host on the public services segment, the attacker could install software to redirect traffic from the outside host directly to the inside host.

Although neither communication violates the rules implemented in the firewall, the outside host has now achieved connectivity to the inside host through the port redirection process on the public services host. An example of a tool that can provide this type of access is Netcat.

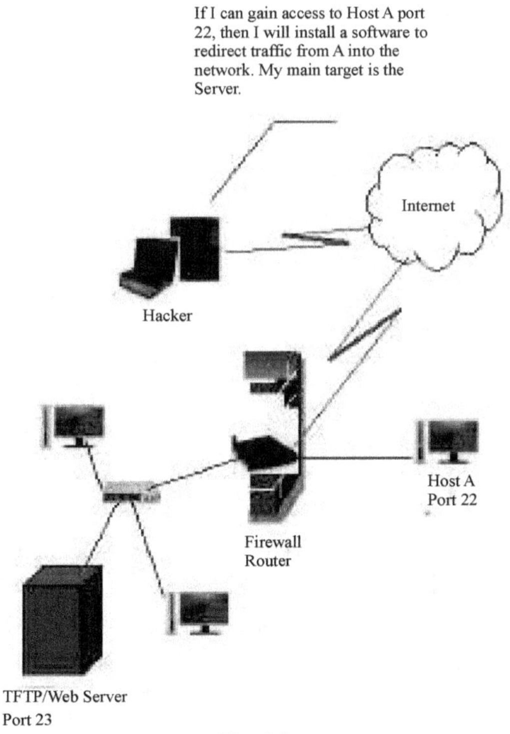

Fig. 8.2

Solution of Port Redirection Attack

Port redirection can be controlled primarily through the use of proper trust models. Antivirus software or a host-based intrusion detection system (IDS) can help detect an attacker and prevent installation of such utilities on a host.

Man-in-the-Middle Attack

A man-in-the-middle (MITM) attack is implemented by intruders that manage to position themselves between two legitimate hosts. The attacker may allow the normal communication between hosts to occur, but manipulates the conversation between the two.

There are many ways that an attacker gets position between two hosts. A very good example is called the transparent proxy. The attacker prey on their victims by sending a phising email or by defacing a legitimate website.

When the victim loads the URL of a defaced webpage, the attackers URL is added to the front of it.

For example: let say http://www.ocbtc.com/ is a legitimate URL. But when website's URL is hacked it becomes http://www.theattacker.com/http://www.ocbtc.com/

If an intruder manages to get into a strategic position, they can steal information, take control of an ongoing session to gain access to private network resources, conduct DoS attacks, corrupt transmitted data, or introduce new information into network sessions.

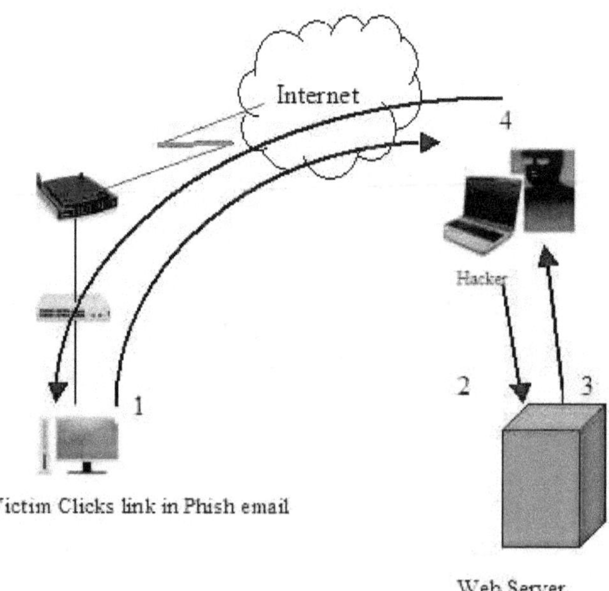

Fig. 8.3

1. When a victim requests a webpage, the host of the victim makes the request to the host of the attacker's.

2. The attacker's host receives the request and fetches the real page from the legitimate website.

3. The attacker can alter the legitimate webpage and apply any transformations to the data they want to make.

4. The attacker forwards the requested page to the victim.

Solutions Man-in-the-Middle Attack

One of the ways to control Man-in-the-middle (MITM) attack is by using VPN tunnels, this allow the attacker to see only the encrypted, unreadable text. These can be especially useful in Wide Area Networks.

In Local Area Networks, attackers use hacking tools such as, ettercap and ARP poisoning. One of the ways to control this type of attack is by configuring port security on LAN switches.

Denial of Service (DoS) Attacks

DoS attack prevents authorized users from using services by consuming system resources. Most times DoS attack is regarded as trivial but in a sense it is a consequentially threat. DoS can cause potential damage to networks. Not only are they easy to execute, but its among the most difficult to eliminate. DoS attacks deserve special attention from network security administrators.

There are different types of DoS attacks. The following are some examples of common DoS threats:

Ping of Death

A ping of death attack gained prominence in the late 1990s. Then were the older operating systems, which were not as secured as the recent ones. Ping of death type of attack took advantage of vulnerabilities or loop holes in older operating systems, what it does was to modified the IP portion of a ping packet header to indicate that there is more data in the packet than there actually was. A ping is normally 64 or 84 bytes, while a ping of death could be up to 65,536 bytes. Sending a ping of this size may crash an older target computer. Most networks are no longer susceptible to this type of attack.

SYN Flood

A SYN flood attack exploits the TCP three-way handshake. It involves sending multiple SYN requests (1,000+) to a targeted server. The server replies with the usual SYN-ACK response, but the malicious host never responds with the final ACK to complete the handshake. This ties up the server until it eventually runs out of resources and cannot respond to a valid host request.

Other types of DoS attacks include:

(*i*) E-mail bombs - Programs send bulk e-mails to individuals, lists, or domains, monopolizing e-mail services.

(*ii*) Malicious applets - These attacks are Java, JavaScript, or ActiveX programs that cause destruction or tie up computer resources.

Distributed DoS

This type of attack is executed by flooding network links with illegitimate data. This data can overwhelm an Internet link, thereby enabling legitimate traffic to be dropped.

Solution of Didtributed DoS

DoS and DDoS attacks can be controlled by the implementation of special anti-spoof and anti-DoS Access Control Lists.

ISPs can also implement traffic rate, limiting the amount of unnecessary traffic that crosses network segments. A common example is to limit the amount of ICMP traffic that is allowed into a network, because this traffic is used only for problem-solving purposes.

Questions

Q.1. What are the types of network attacks. Explain any one?

Q.2. What is network access attacks and what are the types of network access attacks?

Q.3. What is password attack and give the solution for saving this attack?

Q.4. What is trust exploitation attack and give the solution for saving this attack?

Q.5. What is Denial of Services attack and what are the types of Denial of Services attack?

Chapter 9

E-COMMERCE

E-commerce concept has changed a way of doing business in a modern world. It is not just electronic payment on the Internet. There are several application areas in this category; like banking activities, publishing including electronic distribution, sales portals covering sales, marketing, production, management, and distribution. For example one is able to buy an airline ticket, download music or a book just by giving a credit card number and click download button in a webpage, do bid in auction for merchandise. And what's best, you have a 24/7 availability worldwide markets and machines are tireless unlike humans. When enabling these kind of services, protection of a individual privacy, computer security and application technology is are key issues. If security issues are challenged by the users it also means that there will not be users for the services. There are several technologies available for these growing markets saving companies for marketing storage and logistics cost.

Definition

In short "Ecommerce is the process of buying and selling goods over the internet". There is no phusical connectio between the buyer and supplier. In general ecommerce activity include the following-

- Access merchant or vendor site on the cloud / internet.
- Choose

Access merchant site on the cloud / internet

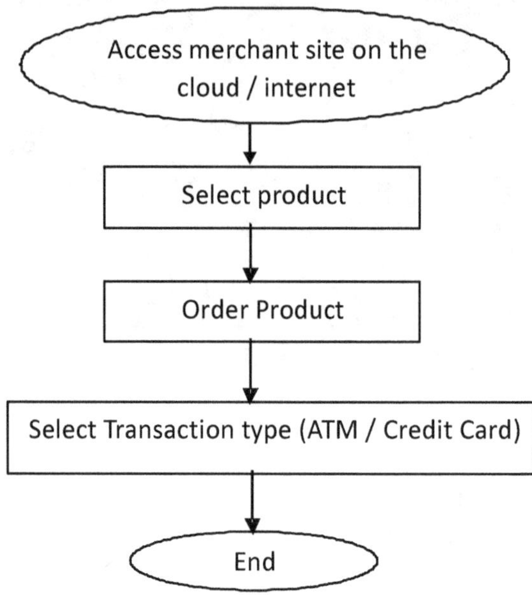

Fig. 9.1

Types of Ecommerce

- Business to- Consumer (B2C)
- Business-to-Business (B2B)
- Consumer-to-Consumer (C2C)
- Business-to-Government (B2G)
- Mobile commerce (m-commerce)

Business to Business (B2B)

When E-Commerce is extended to supply chain management between and among businesses, we get a new concept, which is called Business to business (B2B). B2B area is nowadays growing much faster than B2C and about 80% of the ecommerce is this type. Companies are able to manage different element along the supply chain like manufacturers, distributors and dealers. So B2B e-commerce is simply e-commerce between two or more companies. Main focus in B2B is on procurement where as B2C already focuses on selling and marketing.

There are two distinct aspects of B2B e-commerce that separate it from the more familiar business-to-consumer (B2C): Flexibility in pricing; Transactions between businesses often require variability in the pricing of products between purchasers whereas B2C the price is same for everybody or varies rarely in the B2C marketplace. Integration of business systems; to realize increased productivity and savings, businesses involved in B2B will integrate their internal systems together, enabling less human intervention. B2B on the internet sounds very attempting, but before making any investment in B2B e-commerce, a company must identify the value created and the effort required for implementation under each of the three categories.

C2C e-commerce

Consumer-to-consumer (C2C) e-commerce occurs between private individuals or consumers. Examples of C2C ecommerce are:

- Auctions portals, such as eBay, which allows online real-time bidding on items being sold in the Web;

- Peer-to-peer systems, such as the Kazaa or Napster model where private individual share files containing different kind of data. In Finland it is illegal to share any kind of copyrighted material in peer to networks.

- Different advertising portals like keltainenporssi.fi were individual can sell or buy junk or goods to each other. There are also forums on the Internet, that people can place adds for buying or selling staff related to forum subject.

Business-to-government e-commerce (B2G)

E-Commerce between companies and the public sector is usually referred as Business-to-government ecommerce. In practise it means the use of the Internet for licensing procedures, public procurement, and other government-related operations. In B2G the public sector has a leading role for establishing e-commerce. Which also is based on a need for public sector make its procurement system more effective. Web-based purchasing policies increase the transparency of the procurement process and reduce the risk of irregularities. Nowadays however, the size of the B2G ecommerce portion of the total e-commerce is only small fraction and insignificant.

Mobile Commerce (m-commerce)

Mobile commerce or m-commerce is defined as a process of buying and selling of goods or services through wireless technology. Most common representative in this category is of cause mobile phone. Biggest benefit of m commerce is, that terminal is portable and there is radio coverage in major cities. There is also increasing amount of services available in m-commerce sector for example;

Need of Security in E-Commerce

The six security needs in E-commerce applications are:
- Access Control.
- Confidentiality.

- Authentication.
- Non Repudiation.
- Integrity.
- Availability.

Access Control

Access control ensures only those that authorized require access to resources are given access. This means only the authorized persons are allowed to access the resources.

Confidentiality

When information is copied or read by someone not authorized to do so, the result is known as loss of confidentiality. For some types of information, confidentiality or privacy is a very important attribute. Examples include research data, insurance and medical records, new product specifications, and corporate investment strategies. In some locations, there may be a legal obligation to protect the privacy of the individuals. This is particularly true for loan and bank companies; debt collectors; businesses that extend credit to their customers or issue credit cards; hospitals, doctors' offices, and medical testing laboratories; individuals or agencies that offer services such as psychological counselling or drug treatment; and agencies that collect taxes. Information can be corrupted when it is available on an insecure communication network. When information is modified in unexpected ways, the result is known as loss of the integrity. This means that unauthorized changes are made to information, whether by intentional tampering or human error.

Authentication

In e-Business, computing and information security it is necessary to ensure that the data, transactions, communications or documents (electronic or physical) are genuine. It is also very important for authenticity to validate that both parties involved are who they claim they are.

Non Repudiation

In law, non-repudiation means one's intention to fulfil their obligations to a contract. It also means that one party of a transaction cannot deny having received a transaction nor can the other party deny having sent a transaction. E- commerce uses technology such as digital signatures and encryption to establish authenticity and non- repudiation.

Integrity

Integrity is particularly important for critical safety and financial information used for activities such as electronic funds transfers, air traffic control, and financial accounting. Information can be erased or become inaccessible, resulting in loss of availability. This means that persons who are authorized to get information cannot get what they need.

Availability

For any information system to serve its purpose, the information must be available whenever it is needed. This means that the computing systems used to store and process the information, the security controls used to protect that information, and the communication channels used to access it must be functioning correctly. High availability systems aim to remain available at all times, preventing the service disruptions due to power outages, hardware failures, and system upgrades.

Threats to E-Commerce Security

Authentication Attacks

These types of attacks occur when a user changes system resources or gains access to system information without authorization by either sharing logins or passwords or using an unattended terminal with an open session. Password attack is a frequently used method of repeating attempts on a user account and password. They are performed using a program that runs across a network and attempts to log into a shared resource (for example a server).

Integrity Attacks

In this type of attack, data or information is added, modified, or removed in transit across the network. This requires root access to the router or a system. If a program does not check the buffer limits when reading or receiving data, this opening can be exploited by an attacker to add arbitrary data into a program or system. When running, this data gives the intruder root access to the system. Integrity attacks can create a delay, causing data to be held or otherwise made unavailable for a period of time. The attackers flood the network with useless traffic, making the system extremely slow to serve the customers, and in the extreme case, causing the system to crash down. They could also cause the data to be discarded before the final delivery. Both delay and denial attacks can result in the denial of service(DOS) to the network users.

Confidentiality Attacks

Because network computers communicate serially (even if networks communicate in parallel) and contain limited immediate buffers, data and information are transmitted in small blocks or pieces called packets. The hackers use a variety of methods known collectively as social engineering attacks. With the use of dozens of shareware and freeware packet sniffers available, which do not require the user to understand anything about the underlying protocols, the attackers would capture all network packets and thereby the users login names, passwords, and even accounts. The attackers usually take advantage of human tendency, e.g. using a single, same password for multiple accounts. More often they are successful in gaining access to corporate sensitive and confidential information. Some snooping attacks place the network interface card in promiscuous mode, while the other packet sniffers capture the first 300 bytes of all telnet, file transfer protocol (FTP), and login sessions.

Virus

Viruses are computer programs that are written by devious programmers and are designed to replicate themselves and infect specific computers when triggered by a specific event. For example, viruses called macro viruses attach themselves to files that contain macro instructions (routines that can be repeated automatically, such as mail merges) and are then activated every time when the macro runs. The effects of some viruses are relatively benign and cause annoying interruptions such as displaying the comical message when striking a certain letter on the keyboard. Other viruses are more destructive and cause such problems as deleting files from a hard disk or slowing down a system. A network can be infected by a virus only if the virus enters the network through an outside source- for example through an infected floppy disk or a file downloaded from the Internet. When one computer on the network becomes infected then the other computers on the network are highly susceptible to contracting the virus.

Trojan Horse

A trojan horse is a malicious code which requires users to invite it in, and is therefore disguised as something else. Unsuspecting users will allow the trojan in to their machine through a seemingly harmless and routine task, only to have their system compromised. A typical trojan horse will be presented as something useful such as an e- mail alert regarding a new security patch. The e- mail might provide a link, inviting the user to click on it to download and install the patch. When the link is followed the trojan gains access to the user's computer and then executes its programmed task. By design, a trojan horse is used by hackers to gain access of a large network or secure system so as to put it to use for its own purposes.

Worms

Computer worms are malicious programs designed to spread via computer networks. Computer worms are one form of malware along with the viruses and trojans. A person typically installs worms by inadvertently opening an e- mail attachment or message that contains executable scripts. Once installed on a system, worms spontaneously generate additional email messages contaning copies of the worm. They may also open TCP ports to create networks security holes for other applications, and they may attempt to "flood" the network with spurious Denial of Service (DoS) data transmissions. Being embedded inside everyday network software, computer worms easily penetrate in to most firewalls and other network security measures.

Database Threats

E-commerce systems store user personal data and retrieve product information from databases connected to the web-server. Besides product information, databases connected to the web contain valuable and private information that could irreparably damage a company if it were altered or disclosed. Some databases store username and password pairs in a non-secure way. If someone obtains user authentication information, then he/ she can masquerade as a legitimate database user and reveal private and costly information.

Electronic Payment System

Issues of trust and acceptance play a more significant role in the e-commerce world than in traditional businesses as far as payment systems are concerned.

Traditionally, a customer sees a product, examines it, and then pays for it by cash, check, or credit card. In the e-commerce world, in most cases the customer does not actually see the concrete product at the time of transaction, and the method of payment is performed electronically.

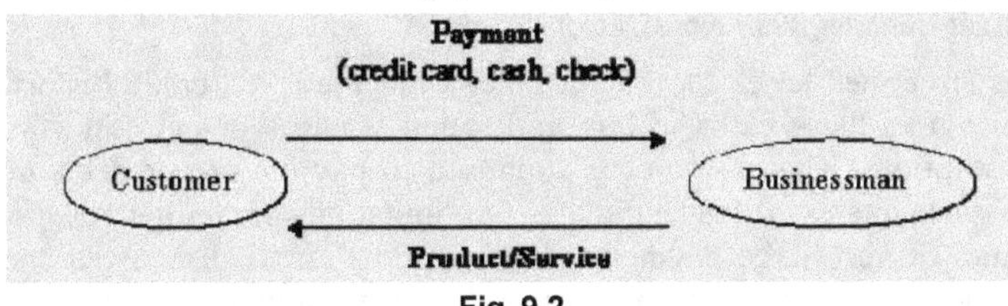

Fig. 9.2

EPSs enable a customer to pay for the goods and services online by using integrated hardware and software systems. The main objectives of EPS are to increase efficiency, improve security, and enhance customer convenience and ease of use.

Terminologies in ecommerce

Electronic funds transfer (EFT): EFT involves electronic transfer of money by financial institutions.

Payment cards : They contain stored financial value that can be transferred from the customer's computer to the businessman's computer.

Credit cards : They are the most popular method used in EPSs and are used by charging against the customer credit.

Smart cards: They include stored financial value and other important personal and financial information used for online payments.

Electronic money (e-money/e-cash): This is standard money converted into an electronic format to pay for online purchases.

Online payment: This can be used for monthly payment for Internet, phone bills, etc.

Electronic wallets (e-wallets) : They are similar to smart cards as they include stored financial value for online payments.

Micro-payment systems : They are similar to e-wallets in that they include stored financial value for online payments; on the other hand, they are used for small payments, such as kurus in Turkey .

Electronic gifts : They are one way of sending electronic currency or gift certificates from one individual to another. The receiver can spend these gifts in their favorite online stores provided they accept this type of currency.

Payment Cards

Credit cards, debit cards, charge cards, smart cards are payment cards. They are the most popular tool for electronic payment transactions.

Credit Cards

There are two types of credit cards on the market today:

- Credit cards issued by credit card companies (e.g., MasterCard, Visa) and major banks (e.g. Is Bankasi, Ziraat Bankasi, Yapi Kredi, etc.)

  Credit cards are issued based on the customer's income level, credit history, and total wealth. The customer uses these cards to buy goods and services or get cashfrom the participating financial institutions. The customer is supposed to pay his or her debts during the payment period; otherwise interest will accumulate. Twolimitations of credit cards are their unsuitability for very small or very large payments. It is not cost-justified to use a credit card for small payments. Also, dueto security issues, these cards have a limit and cannot be used for excessively large transactions.

- Credit cards issued by department stores (e.g Boyner), oil companies (e.g. Shell) Businesses extremely benefit from these company cards and they are cheaper to operate. They are widely issued to and used by a broad range of customers.

Debit Cards

The difference between credit cards and debit cards is that in order to pay with a debit card you need to know your personal identification number (PIN) and need a hardware device that is able to read the information that is stored in the magnetic strip on the back.

Debit cards task similar to checks in that the charges will be taken from the customer's checking account. The benefit for the customer is the easiness of use and convenience. These cards also keep the customer under his or her budget because they do not allow the customer to go beyond his or her resources. The advantage to the merchant is the speed at which the merchant collects these charges.

Charge Cards

Charge cards are similar to credit cards except they have no revolving credit line, so the balance must be paid off every month. Credit, debit, and charge card methods of payments have been successfully utilized in the pre-Internet period, and they are often used in the e-commerce world as well. Some of the reasons for their popularity in the e-commerce world are their availability (most customers own one of these cards), ease of use, and acceptance. To use these cards as an online payment system, a well-defined process is followed. A brief description follows.

To accept payment cards payments, a merchant must have a merchant account with a bank. The buyer will be required to submit their credit-card number, expiration date and shipping and billing information when making a purchase online using a payment card. (Figure 4.3) A customer using his/her browser clicks on a product on the merchant's web site and adds it to an electronic shopping cart. The customer provides the shipping instructions and payment card information. This information is sent securely over the Internet to the merchant's commerce site .The server software adds the merchant identification to the information

transmitted. The merchant then submits this information to the acquiring bank with which the merchant holds an account (Step 2). The merchant bank transmits this information to the customer's bank for authorization. Then, the buyer's account information is verified. This involves the issuing bank from which the buyer obtained the credit card, and the credit-card association (Step 3). Verification is received by the acquiring bank (Step 4) and is passed on to the merchant (Step 5) who then ships the product (Step 6). Payment cannot be issued to the merchant until the product has been shipped. This entire process (not including shipment) takes approximately less than 30 seconds.

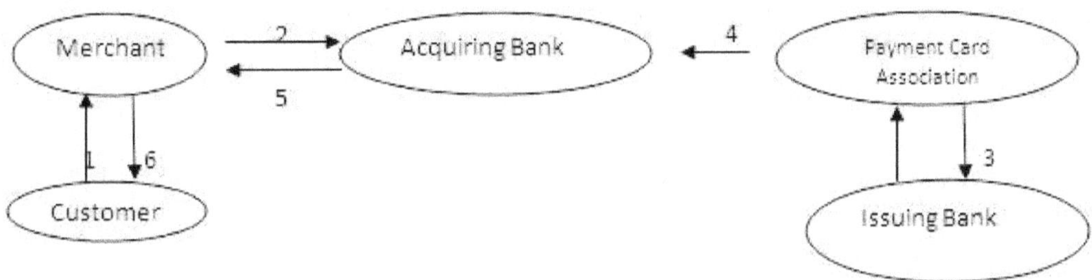

Fig- Online payment card system

Electronic Cash (E-cash)

Similar to regular cash, e-cash enables transactions between customers without the need for banks or other third parties. When used, e-cash is transferred directly and immediately to the participating merchants and vending machines. Electronic cash is a secure and convenient alternative to bills and coins. This payment system complements credit, debit, and charge cards and adds additional convenience and control to everyday customer cash transactions. E-cash usually operates on a smart card, which includes an embedded microprocessor chip. The microprocessor chip stores cash value and the security features that make electronic transactions secure.

E-cash is transferred directly from the customer's desktop to the merchant's site. Therefore, e-cash transactions usually require no remote authorization or personal identification number (PIN) codes at the point of sale. E-cash can be transferred over a telephone line or over the Web. The microprocessor chip embedded onto the card keeps track of the e-cash transactions. Using e-cash the customer has two options: a stand-alone card containing e-cash or a combination card that incorporates both e-cash and debit .

Electronic Cheque (e-cheque)

E-check is the result of cooperation among several banks, government entities, technology companies, and e-commerce organizations. An e-check uses the same legal and business protocols associated with traditional paper checks. It is a new payment instrument that combines high-security, speed, convenience, and processing efficiencies for online transactions. It shares the speed and processing efficiencies of all-electronic payments. An e-check can be used by large and small organizations, even where other electronic payment solutions are too risky or not appropriate. The key advantages of e-checks are as follows:

- Secure and quick settlement of financial obligations
- Fast check processing
- Very low transaction cost

Secure EPS Infrastructure

Secure electronic funds transfer is crucial to e-commerce. In order to ensure the integrity and security of each electronic transaction and other EPSs utilize some or all of the following security measures and technologies directly related to EPSs:

- Authentication
- Public key cryptography
- Digital Signature
- Certificate

Authentication

This is the process of verification of the authenticity of a person and/or a transaction. There are many tools available to confirm the authenticity of a user. For instance, passwords and ID numbers are used to allow a user to log onto a particular site.

Public Key Cryptography

Public key cryptography uses two keys , one public and one private , to encrypt and decrypt data, respectively. Cryptography is the process of protecting the integrity and accuracy of information by encrypting data into an unreadable format, called cipher text. Only those who possess a private key can decrypt the message into plain text.

Public key cryptography uses a pair of keys, one private and one public. In contrast, private key cryptography uses only one key for encryption. The advantage of the dual-key technique is that it allows the businesses to give away their public key to anyone who wants to send a message. The sender can then encrypt the message with the public key and send it to the intended businessman over the Internet or any other public network; the businessman can then use the private key to decrypt the message. Obviously, the private key is not publicly known.

Digital Signature

Rather than a written signature that can be used by an individual to authenticate the identity of the sender of a message or of the signer of a document; a digital signature is an electronic one. E-check technology also allows digital signatures to be applied to document blocks, rather than to the entire document. This lets part of a document to be separated from the original, without compromising the integrity of the digital signature. This technology would also be very useful for business contracts and other legal documents transferred over the Web. Private key that is able to identify the origin of the message. The followings are some functions of digital signature.

- **The authentication function:** The term digital signature in general is relevant to the practice of adding a string of characters to an electronic message that serves to identify the sender or the originator of a message.

- **The seal function:** Some digital signature techniques also serve to provide a check against any alteration of the text of the message after the digital signature was appended.

- **The integrity function:** This function is of great interest in cases where legal documents are created using such digital signatures.

- **The privacy function:** Privacy and confidentiality are of significan concerns in many instances where the sender wishes to keep the contents of the message private from all hut the intended recipient

Certificate

A driver's license is accepted by numerous organizations both public and private as a form of identification due to the legitimacy of the issuer, which is a government agency. Since organizations understand the process by which someone can obtain a driver's license, they can trust that the issuer verified the identity of the individual to whom the license was issued. A certificate provides a mechanism for establishing confidence in the relationship between a public key and the entity that owns the corresponding private key.

Certificate Authorities

Certificate authorities are similar to a notary public, a commonly trusted third party. In the e-commerce world, certificate authorities are the corresponding of passport offices in the government that concern digital certificates and validate the holder's identity and authority.

Questions

Q.1. Define E-Commerce and what are the types of E-commerce, Explain it?

Q.2. Define Mobile Commerce or m-commerce and what are the needs of security in E-Commerce?

Q.3. Write a short notes of the following:

    (*i*) Payment Card   (*ii*) Credit Card   (*iii*) E-Cash   (*iv*) E-Cheque

    (*v*) Micro Payment System   (*vi*) Debit Card

Q.4. What is Electronic Payment System, Explain it?

Q.5. What is digital signature and give the functions of digital signature?

Chapter 10

PHYSICAL SECURITY OF IT ASSET

"Physical security" is almost everything that happens before you (or an attacker) start typing commands on the keyboard. It's the alarm system that calls the police department when a late-night thief tries to break into your building. It's the key lock on the computer's power supply that makes it harder for unauthorized people to turn the machine off. And it's the surge protector that keeps a computer from being damaged by power surges.

Protecting Computer Hardware

There are several measures that you can take to protect your computer system against physical threats. Many of them will simultaneously protect the system from dangers posed by nature, outsiders, and inside saboteurs.

The Environment

Computers are extremely complicated devices that often require exactly the right balance of physical and environmental conditions to properly operate. Altering this balance can cause your computer to fail in unexpected and often undesirable ways. Even worse, your computer might continue to operate, but erratically, producing incorrect results and corrupting valuable data.

Fire

Computers are notoriously bad at surviving fires. If the flames don't cause your system's case and circuit boards to ignite, the heat might melt your hard drive and all the solder holding the electronic components in place. Your computer might even survive the fire, only to be destroyed by the water used to fight the flames.

Smoke

Smoke is very good at damaging computer equipment. Smoke is a potent abrasive and collects on the heads of magnetic disks, optical disks, and tape drives. A single smoke particle can cause a several disk crash on some kinds of older disk drives without a sealed drive compartment.

Sometimes smoke is generated by computers themselves. Electrical fires - particularly those caused by the transformers in video monitors - can produce a pungent, acrid smoke that can damage other equipment and may also be a potent carcinogen. Several years ago, a laboratory at Stanford had to be evacuated because of toxic smoke caused by a fire in a single video monitor.

Dust

Dust destroys data. As with smoke, dust can collect on the heads of magnetic disks, tape drives, and optical drives. Dust is abrasive and will slowly destroy both the recording head and the media.

Most dust is electrically conductive. The design of many computers sucks large amounts of air and dust through the computer's insides for cooling. Invariably, a layer of dust will accumulate on a computer's circuit boards, covering every surface, exposed and otherwise. Eventually, the dust will cause circuits to short and fail.

Earthquake

While some parts of the world are subject to frequent and severe earthquakes, nearly every part of the world experiences the occasional temblor. In the United States, for example, the San Francisco Bay Area experiences several earthquakes every year; a major earthquake is expected within the next 20 years that may be equal in force to the great San Francisco earthquake of 1906. Scientists also predict an 80% chance that the eastern half of the United States may experience a similar earthquake within the next 30 years: the only truly unknown factor is where it will occur. As a result, several Eastern cities have enacted stringent anti-earthquake building codes. These days, many new buildings in Boston are built with diagonal cross-braces, using construction that one might expect to see in San Francisco.

Explosion

Although computers are not prone to explosion, the buildings in which they are located can be - especially if a building is equipped with natural gas or is used to store flammable solvents.

If you need to operate a computer in an area where there is a risk of explosion, you might consider purchasing a system with a ruggedized case. Disk drives can be shock-mounted within a computer; if explosion is a constant hazard, consider using a ruggedized laptop with an easily removed, shock-resistant hard drive.

Temperature Extremes

As with people, computers operate best within certain temperature ranges. Most computer systems should be kept between 50 and 90 degrees Fahrenheit (10 to 32 degrees Celsius). If the ambient temperature around your computer gets too high, the computer cannot adequately cool itself, and internal components can be damaged. If the temperature gets too cold, the system can undergo thermal shock when it is turned on, causing circuit boards or integrated circuits to crack.

Bugs (biological)

Sometimes insects and other kinds of bugs find their way into computers. Indeed, the very term bug, used to describe something wrong with a computer program, dates back to the 1950s, when Grace Murray Hopper found a moth trapped between the relay contacts on Harvard University's Mark 1 computer.

Insects have a strange predilection for getting trapped between the high-voltage contacts of switching power supplies. Others seem to have insatiable cravings for the insulation that covers wires carrying line current and the high-pitched whine that switching power supplies emit. Spider webs inside computers collect dust like a magnet.

Electrical Noise

Motors, fans, heavy equipment, and even other computers can generate electrical noise that can cause intermittent problems with the computer you are using. This noise can be transmitted through space or nearby power lines.

Electrical surges are a special kind of electrical noise that consists of one (or a few) high-voltage spikes. As we've mentioned, an ordinary vacuum cleaner plugged into the same electrical outlet as a workstation can generate a spike capable of destroying the workstation's power supply.

Lightning

Lightning generates large power surges that can damage even computers whose electrical supplies are otherwise protected. If lightning strikes your building's metal frame (or hits your building's lightning rod), the resulting current on its way to ground can generate an intense magnetic field.

Vibration

Vibration can put an early end to your computer system by literally shaking it apart. Even gentle vibration, over time, can work printed circuit boards out of their edge connectors, and integrated circuits out of their sockets. Vibration can cause hard disk drives to come out of alignment and increase the chance for catastrophic failure - and resulting data loss.

Humidity

Humidity is your computer's friend - but as with all friends, you can get too much of a good thing. Humidity prevents the buildup of static charge. If your computer room is too dry, static discharge between operators and your computer (or between the computer's moving parts) may destroy information or damage your computer itself. If the computer room is too humid, you may experience condensation on the computer's circuitry, which can short out and damage the electrical circuits.

Water

Water can destroy your computer. The primary danger is an electrical short, which can happen if water bridges between a circuit-board trace carrying voltage and a trace carrying ground. A short will cause too much current to be pulled through a trace, and will heat up the trace and possibly melt it. Shorts can also destroy electronic components by pulling too much current through them.

Environmental Monitoring

To detect spurious problems, you should continuously monitor and record your computer room's temperature and relative humidity. As a general rule of thumb, every 1,000 square feet of office space should have its own recording equipment. Log and check recordings on a regular basis.

Preventing Accidents

In addition to environmental problems, your computer system is vulnerable to a multitude of accidents. While it is impossible to prevent all accidents, careful planning can minimize the impact of accidents that will inevitably occur.

Food and drink

People need food and drink to stay alive. Computers, on the other hand, need to stay away from food and drink. One of the fastest ways of putting a keyboard out of commission is to pour a soft drink or cup of coffee between the keys. If this keyboard is your system console, you may be unable to reboot the computer until the console is replaced (we know this from experience).

Physical Access

Simple common sense will tell you to keep your computer in a locked room. But how safe is that room? Sometimes a room that appears to be quite safe is actually wide open.

Raised floors and Dropped Ceilings

In many modern office buildings, internal walls do not extend above dropped ceilings or beneath raised floors. This type of construction makes it easy for people in adjoining rooms, and sometimes adjoining offices, to gain access.

Entrance Through Air Ducts

If the air ducts that serve your computer room are large enough, intruders can use them to gain entrance to an otherwise secured area.

Glass walls

Although glass walls and large windows frequently add architectural panache, they can be severe security risks. Glass walls are easy to break; a brick and a bottle of gasoline thrown through a window can do an incredible amount of damage. Glass walls are also easy to look through: an attacker can gain critical knowledge, such as passwords or information about system operations, simply by carefully watching people on the other side of a glass wall or window.

Vandalism

Computer systems are good targets for vandalism. Reasons for vandalism include:

- Intentional disruption of services (e.g., a student who has homework due)
- Revenge (e.g., a fired employee)
- Riots
- Strike-related violence
- Entertainment for the feebleminded

Computer vandalism is often fast, easy, and very expensive. Sometimes, vandalism is actually sabotage presented as random vandalism.

Ventilation holes

Several years ago, 60 workstations at the Massachusetts Institute of Technology were destroyed in a single evening by a student who poured Coca-Cola into each computer's ventilation holes. Authorities surmised that the vandal was a student who had not completed a problem set due the next day.

Computers that have ventilation holes need them. Don't seal up the holes to prevent this sort of vandalism. However, a rigidly enforced policy against food and drink in the computer room - or a 24-hour guard - can help prevent this kind of incident from happening at your site.

Network cables

Local and wide area networks are exceedingly vulnerable to vandalism. In many cases, a vandal can disable an entire subnet of workstations by cutting a single wire with a pair of wire cutters. Compared with Ethernet, fiber optic cables are at the same time more vulnerable (because sometimes they can be more easily damaged), more difficult to repair (because fiber optics are difficult to splice), and more attractive targets (because they often carry more information).

Network connectors

In addition to cutting a cable, a vandal who has access to a network's endpoint - a network connector - can electronically disable or damage the network. Ethernet is especially vulnerable to grounding and network-termination problems. Simply by removing a terminator at the end of the network cable or by grounding an Ethernet's inside conductor, an attacker can render the entire network inoperable. Usually this event happens by accident; however, it can also happen as the result of an intentionally destructive attack.

Defending Against Acts of War and Terrorism

Unless your computer is used by the military or being operated in a war zone, it is unlikely to be a war target. Nevertheless, if you live in a region that is subject to political strife, you may wish to consider additional structural protection for your computer room.

Preventing Theft

Because many computers are relatively small and valuable, they are easily stolen and easily sold. Even computers that are relatively difficult to fence - such as DEC VaxStations - have been stolen by thieves who thought that they were actually stealing PCs. As with any expensive piece of equipment, you should attempt to protect your computer investment with physical measures such as locks and bolts.

RAM Theft

Fig. 10.1: SIMMs (Standard inline Memory Modules) are Vulnerable to Theft

In recent years, businesses and universities have suffered a rash of RAM thefts. Thieves enter offices, open computers, and remove some or all of the computer's RAM. Many computer businesses and universities have also had major thefts of advanced processor chips.

RAM and late-model CPU chips are easily sold on the open market. They are untraceable. And, when thieves steal only some of the RAM inside a computer, many weeks or months may pass before the theft is noticed.

Remember, high-density RAM modules and processor cards are worth substantially more than their weight in gold. If a user complains that a computer is suddenly running more slowly than it did the day before, check its RAM, and then check to see that its case is physically secured.

Physically secure your computer

A variety of physical tie-down devices are available to bolt computers to tables or cabinets. Although they cannot prevent theft, they can make theft more difficult.

Encryption

If your computer is stolen, the information it contains will be at the mercy of the equipment's new "owners." They may erase it. Alternatively, they may read it. Sensitive information can be sold, used for blackmail, or used to compromise other computer systems.

You can never make something impossible to steal. But you can make stolen information virtually useless - provided that it is encrypted and that the thief does not know the encryption key. For this reason, even with the best computer-security mechanisms and physical deterrents, sensitive information should be encrypted using an encryption system that is difficult to break. We recommend that you acquire and use a strong encryption system so that even if your computer is stolen, the sensitive information it contains will not be compromised.

Portables

Portable computers present a special hazard. They are easily stolen, difficult to tie down (they then cease to be portable!), and often quite easily resold. Personnel with laptops should be trained to be especially vigilant in protecting their computers. In particular, theft of laptops in airports is a major problem.

Note that theft of laptops may not be motivated by greed (resale potential) alone. Often, competitive intelligence is more easily obtained by stealing a laptop with critical information than by hacking into a protected network. Thus, good encryption on a portable computer is critical. Unfortunately, this encryption makes the laptop a **"monition"** and difficult to legally remove from many countries (including the U.S.).

Minimizing Downtime

We hope your computer will never be stolen or damaged. But if it is, you should have a plan for immediately securing temporary computer equipment and for loading your backups onto the new systems. This plan is known as disaster recovery.

We recommend that you do the following:

- Establish a plan for rapidly acquiring new equipment in the event of theft, fire, or equipment failure.

- Test this plaMinimizing downtimen by renting (or borrowing) a computer system and trying to restore your backups.

Related Concerns

Beyond the items mentioned earlier, you may also wish to consider the impact on your computer center of the following:

- Loss of phone service or networks. How will this impact your regular operations?
- Vendor going bankrupt. How important is support? Can you move to another hardware or software system?
- Significant absenteeism. Will this impact your ability to operate?
- Death or incapacitation of key personnel. Can every member of your computer organization be replaced?
- What are the contingency plans?

Protecting Data

Obviously, as described above, there is a strong overlap between physical security and data privacy and integrity. Indeed, the goal of some attacks is not the physical destruction of your computer system but the penetration and removal (or copying) of the sensitive information it contains. This section explores several different types of attacks on data and discusses approaches for protecting against these attacks.

Eavesdropping

Electronic eavesdropping is perhaps the most sinister type of data piracy. Even with modest equipment, an eavesdropper can make a complete transcript of a victim's actions - every keystroke, and every piece of information viewed on a screen or sent to a printer. The victim, meanwhile, usually knows nothing of the attacker's presence, and blithely goes about his or her work, revealing not only sensitive information, but the passwords and procedures necessary for obtaining even more.

In many cases, you cannot possibly know if you're being monitored. Sometimes you will learn of an eavesdropper's presence when the attacker attempts to make use of the information obtained: often, by then, you cannot prevent significant damage. With care and vigilance, however, you can significantly decrease the risk of being monitored.

Wiretapping

By their very nature, electrical wires are prime candidates for eavesdropping (hence the name wiretapping). An attacker can follow an entire conversation over a pair of wires with a simple splice - sometimes he doesn't even have to touch the wires physically: a simple induction loop coiled around a terminal wire is enough to pick up most voice and RS-232 communications.

Here are some guidelines for preventing wiretapping:

- Routinely inspect all wires that carry data (especially terminal wires and telephone lines used for modems) for physical damage.

- Protect your wires from monitoring by using shielded cable. Armored cable provides additional protection.

- If you are very security conscious, place your cables in steel conduit. In high-security applications, the conduit can be pressurized with gas; gas pressure monitors can be used to trip an alarm system in the event of tampering. However, these approaches are notoriously expensive to install and maintain.

Protecting Backups

Backups should be a prerequisite of any computer operation - secure or otherwise - but the information stored on backup tapes is extremely vulnerable. When the information is stored on a computer, the operating system's mechanisms of checks and protections prevents unauthorized people from viewing the data (and can possibly log failed attempts). After information is written onto a backup tape, anybody who has physical possession of the tape can read its contents.

For this reason, protect your backups at least as well as you normally protect your computers themselves.

Here are Some Guidelines for Protecting Your Backups:

- Don't leave backups hanging unattended in a computer room that is generally accessible. Somebody could take a backup and then have access to all of the files on your system.

- Don't entrust backups to a messenger who is not bonded.

- Sanitize backup tapes before you sell them, use them as scratch tapes, or otherwise dispose of them.

Verify Your Backups

Verify backups that are months or years old in addition to backups that were made yesterday or the week before. Sometimes, backups in archives are slowly erased by environmental conditions. Magnetic tape is also susceptible to a process called print through, in which the magnetic domains on one piece of tape wound on a spool affects the next layer.

The only way to find out if this process is harming your backups is to test them periodically. You can also minimize print through by spinning your tapes to the end and then rewinding them, because the tape will not line back up in the same way when the tape is rewound. We recommend that at least once a year, you check a sample of your backup tapes to make sure that they contain valid data.

Protect Your Backups

Many of the hazards to computers mentioned in the first part of this chapter are equally hazardous to backups. To maximize the chances of your data surviving in the event of an accident or malicious incident, keep your computer system and your backups in different locations.

Sanitize Your Media Before Disposal

If you throw out your tapes, or any other piece of recording media, be sure that the data on the tapes has been completely erased. This process is called sanitizing.

Simply deleting a file that is on your hard disk doesn't delete the data associated with the file. Parts of the original data - and sometimes entire files - can usually be easily recovered. When you are disposing of old media, be sure to destroy the data itself, in addition to the directory entries.

Backup Encryption

Backup security can be substantially enhanced by encrypting the data stored on the backup tapes. Many Macintosh and PC backup packages provide for encrypting a backup set; some of these programs even use decent encryption algorithms. (Do not trust a backup system's encryption if the program's manufacturer refuses to disclose the algorithm.) Several tape drive manufacturers sell hardware that contains chips that automatically encrypt all data as it is written. We discuss the issue of encrypting your backups.

Protecting Local Storage

In addition to computers and mass-storage systems, many other pieces of electrical data-processing equipment store information. For example, terminals, modems and laser printers often contain pieces of memory that may be downloaded and uploaded with appropriate control sequences.

Naturally, any piece of memory that is used to hold sensitive information presents a security problem, especially if that piece of memory is not protected with a password, encryption, or other similar mechanism. However, the local storage in many devices presents an additional security problem, because sensitive information is frequently copied into such local storage without the knowledge of the computer user.

Questions

Q.1. What is the meaning of Physical Security and what are the use of Physical Security?

Q.2. What are the methods use for protecting the computer hardware?

Q.3. What are the methods use for defending against acts of war and terrorism?

Q.4. How will we verify our backup verify?

Q.5. Define Protecting Backups?

Q.6. Write a short notes of the following:

    (i) RAM Theft

    (ii) Wiretapping

    (iii) Eavesdropping

    (iv) Ventilation Hole

Chapter 11

INTRUSION DETECTION SYSTEM

Intrusion-detection systems aim at detecting attacks against computer systems and networks or, in general, against information systems. Sometimes, it is difficult to provide provably secure information systems and to maintain them in such a secure state during their lifetime and utilization. Therefore, intrusion detection systems have the task of monitoring the usage of such systems to detect any apparition of insecure states. They detect attempts and active misuse either by legitimate users of the information systems or by external parties to abuse their privileges or exploit security vulnerabilities.

Efficiency of intrusion-detection systems

To evaluate the efficiency of an intrusion-detection system:

Accuracy: Accuracy deals with the proper detection of attacks and the absence of false alarms. Inaccuracy occurs when an intrusion-detection system ags a legitimate action in the environment as anomalous or intrusive.

Performance: The performance of an intrusion-detection system is the rate at which audit events are processed. If the performance of the intrusion-detection system is poor, then real-time detection is not possible.

Completeness: Completeness is the property of an intrusion-detection system to detect all attacks. Incompleteness occurs when the intrusion-detection system fails to detect an attack. This measure is much more difficult to evaluate than the others because it is impossible to have a global knowledge about attacks or abuses of privileges.

"The process of monitoring the events occurring in a computer system or network and analyzing them for signs of *intrusion*."

Types of Intrusion Detection System:–

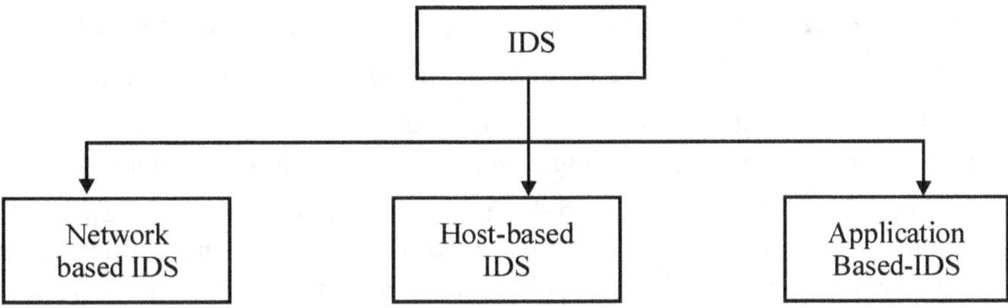

Network-based IDS

The network IDS usually has two logical components:

- the sensor and

- the management station.

The sensor sits on a network segment, monitoring it for suspicious traffic.

The management station receives alarms from the sensor(s) and displays them to an operator.

The sensors are usually dedicated systems that exist only to monitor the network. They have an network interface in promiscuous mode, which means they receive all network traffic, not just that destined for their IP address, and they capture passing network traffic for analysis. If they detect something that looks unusual, they pass it back to the analysis station.

The analysis station can display the alarms or do additional analysis. Some displays are simply an interface to a network management tool, like HP Open view, but some are custom GUIs designed to help the operator analyze the problem.

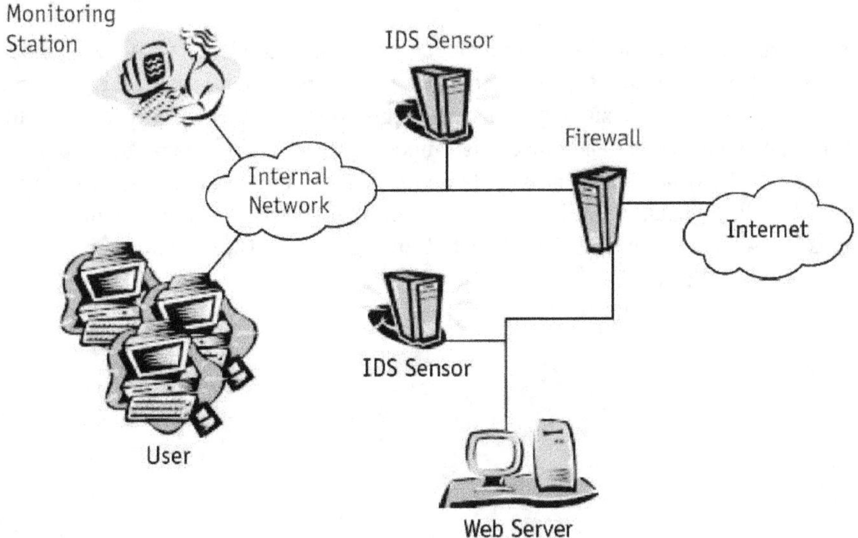

Strengths

The network intrusion detection systems can detect some of the attacks that use the network. They are good for detecting access without authority or some kinds of access in excess of authority.

A network-based IDS does not require modification of production servers or hosts.

This is an advantage because production servers frequently have close operating tolerances for CPU, Input Output, and disk capacity; installing additional software may exceed the systems capacities.

The IDS is not on a critical path for any production services or processes because a network-based IDS does not act as a router or other critical device. System failure does not have a significant impact on the business. A side benefit of this is that you are likely to encounter less resistance from other people within your organization; the risk to existing critical processes is lower with a network system than with a host system.

Network-based IDS systems tend to be more self-contained than host-based systems.

They run on a dedicated system that is simple to install; merely unbox the device, do some remedial configuration, and plug it into your network in a location that permits it to monitor sensitive traffic.

Weaknesses

A network based IDS, on the other hand, only examine network traffic on the segment to which it is directly connected, but it cannot detect an attack that travels through a different network segment. This problem—localized vision—is particularly endemic in a switched ethernet environment. The problem may require that an organization purchase many sensors in order to meet their network coverage goals. Since each sensor costs money, broad coverage with network IDS sensors can become prohibitively expensive.

Network intrusion detection systems tend to use signature analysis in order to meet performance requirements. This will detect common programmed attacks from external sources, but it is inadequate for detecting more complex information threats. This requires a more robust ability to examine the environment.

A network intrusion detection system may need to communicate large volumes of data back to the central analysis system. Sometimes that means that any given monitored packet generates a larger amount of analysis traffic. Many such systems use aggressive data-reduction processes to reduce the amount of communicated traffic. They also push much of the decision-making processes out into the sensor itself and use the central station as a status display or communications center, rather than for actual analysis. The disadvantage of this is that it provides very little coordination amongst sensors; any given sensor is unaware that another has detected an attack. Such a system cannot normally detect synergistic or complex attacks.

Network-based IDS may have a difficult time handling attacks within encrypted sessions. Fortunately, there are very few attacks that take place within an encrypted traffic session, other than attacks against weak web servers. This will become more of an issue as organizations transition to IPv6.

Host based IDS

The host-based IDS looks for signs of intrusion on the local host system. These frequently use the host system's audit and logging mechanism as a source of information for analysis.

They look for unusual activity that is confined to the local host such as logins, improper file access, unapproved privilege escalation, or alterations on system privileges. This IDS architecture generally uses rule-based engines for analyzing activity; an example of such a rule might be, "superuser privilege can only be attained through the su command." Therefore successive login attempts to the *root* account might be considered an attack.

Strengths

Host-based IDS can be an extremely powerful tool for analyzing a possible attack. For example, it can sometimes tell exactly what the attacker did, which commands he ran, what files he opened, and what system calls he executed, rather than just a rather vague accusation that an he attempted to execute a dangerous command. A host-based IDS usually provides much more detailed and relevant information than a network-based IDS.

Host-based systems tend to have lower false positive rates than do network-based systems. This happens because the range of commands executed on a specific host is much more focused than the types of traffic flowing across a network. This property can reduce the complexity of host based analysis engines.

Host based systems can be used in environments where broad intrusion detection is not needed, or where the bandwidth is not available for sensor-to-analysis communications.

Host based systems can be completely self-contained. This also allows host-based systems to run, in some cases, from read-only media; this prevents the attackers from disabling the IDS.

Finally, a host-based system may be less risky to configure with an active response, such as terminating a service or logging off an offending user. A host based system is more difficult to spoof into restricting access from legitimate sources.

Weaknesses

Host-based systems require installation on the particular device that you wish to protect. If, for example, you have a human resources server, and you want to protect it, you have to install the IDS on that server. As mentioned earlier, this can pose capacity problems. In some cases, it can even pose security problems, since the security personnel may not ordinarily have access to the server in question.

Another problem associated with host-based systems is that they tend to rely on the innate logging and monitoring capabilities of the server. If the server isn't configured to do adequate logging and monitoring, you have to change the configuration of, possibly, a production machine, which is a tremendous change management problem.

How do you adequately predict the results of adding that logging capability?

Host-based systems are relatively expensive. Many organizations do not have the financial resources to protect entire network segments using host-based systems.

These organizations must very carefully choose which systems to protect. This can leave wide gaps in ID coverage, because, for example, an attacker on a neighboring but unprotected system can sniff authentication information or other sensitive material from the network.

Finally, host-based systems suffer, to an even greater degree, from local-vision restrictions. They are almost totally ignorant of the network environment. Thus, the analysis time required to evaluate damage from a potential intrusion increases linearly with the number of protected hosts; i.e., if a human takes time t to investigate an incident on one system, it will take **2t** to investigate two systems, **3t** to investigate three systems, and so forth.

File Integrity Checkers

A file integrity checker examines the files on a computer to determine whether they\ have been altered since the last time the integrity checker was run. The integrity checker keeps a database of hash values for each file. Each time the checker runs, it recalculates the hash value and compares it to the stored value. If the hash values are different, the file has changed. If the values are not different, the file has not changed.

Strengths

It is computationally infeasible to defeat the mathematics in an integrity checker. This makes it a very, very strong tool for detecting changes to files on a computer. It is so strong, in fact, that it is one of the most important tools you can use to detect misuse of computer systems.

Integrity checkers can be configured to watch everything on the system, or only important files. They are extremely flexible.

Once attackers compromise a system, they like to do two things. First, they like to cover up their tracks, which means that they will alter system binaries, libraries, or log files to hide the fact that they are or have been on the system. Second, they will make changes to ensure they will have continued access to the system. A properly configured file integrity checker will detect both activities.

Weaknesses

Integrity checkers rely on data stored on the local computers. Like log files, this data (the database of hash values) is vulnerable to modification on the system. Say an attacker gains super user privileges on your system. The attacker can find the integrity checker, make any hostile changes to the system, and re-run the integrity checker to recreate the database of hash values. When the system administrator runs the tool, it will not report any changes to the system.

One way around this problem is to keep your database on read-only media such as a writable CD. This works for mostly stable and unchanging systems, but for most nproduction machines it is incredibly inconvenient.

The integrity checker must be configured for each system. Usually this is a time-consuming and complicated task. If the operating system is not good at enforcing system integrity, installation becomes even more complex.

Once the checker is configured, it must be run frequently. Depending on the operating system, simple changes or normal operation can report from tens to thousands of changes.

For example, an integrity checker run just before upgrading MS-Outlook on a Windows NT system, then just after the installation, reported over 1800 changes.

Finally, integrity checkers consume a considerable number of system resources." They can check CPU, memory, and disk space. Many administrators will not want to run integrity checkers frequently. This limits their functionality, because a checker run once a month will report so many changes that a real attack has a good chance of going unnoticed.

Vulnerability Scanners

A vulnerability scanner differs from an intrusion detection system, as mentioned earlier, in that the vulnerability scanner looks for static configurations and the IDS looks for transient misuse or abnormalities. A vulnerability scanner may look for a known NFS vulnerability by examining the available services and configuration on a remote system. An IDS, handling the same vulnerability, would only report the existence of the vulnerability when an attacker attempted to exploit it.

Network Vulnerability Scanner

A network vulnerability scanner operates remotely by examining the network interface on a remote system. It will look for vulnerable services running on that remote machine, and report on a possible vulnerability. For example, it is well-known that **rexd** is a weak service; a network vulnerability scanner will attempt to connect to the **rexd** service on the target system. If the connection succeeds, the scanner will report a **rexd** vulnerability.

Strengths

Network vulnerability scanners can report on a variety of target architectures. Some work with routers, some with Unix systems, and some with NT or other Windows platforms.

Network vulnerability scanners are, in general, very easy to install and begin using (from a technical standpoint). Unlike host-based systems, which usually require software installation or reconfiguration, a network-based system can be dropped into place on a network. Simply plug the interface into the switch and boot up the machine.

The GUI with a network system tends to be quite intuitive, which means that junior personnel can monitor the system and call more senior analysts if something unusual crops up.

Weaknesses

Network vulnerability scanners are almost exclusively signature-based systems. Like a signature-based IDS, a signature-based vulnerability scanner can only detect those vulnerabilities it is programmed to recognize. If a new vulnerability comes into play, as they frequently do, there is a window of opportunity for the attacker before the vendor updates the signatures (and the customer downloads and installs the new signatures). If the vulnerability remains closely held, systems can remain vulnerable to attack for long periods of time.

If customers are as negligent with their vulnerability scanner signatures as history shows they are with virus signatures, then many organizations will be vulnerable to attack, even though they run vulnerability scanners at regular intervals. A recent analysis showed that 90 percent of web servers running IIS are still vulnerable to a well-documented and very serious security vulnerability, for which the vendor has produced a patch and a security advisory. A vulnerability scanner can only point out possible problems; the organization must still fix them.

Another potential problem with a network vulnerability scanner is that the output still requires skilled interpretation. Every environment has different operating requirements and different security vulnerabilities. In fact, the concept of "vulnerability" embodies other loosely-defined concepts, such as risk, threat, acceptability, and expected attacker skills. Since each of these varies with each organization, the degree to which a particular configuration represents a "vulnerability" also varies with each organization.

When the vulnerability scanner reports a particular vulnerability, the organization's network or operations personnel must evaluate that report within the context of the organization's operating environment. The vulnerability may not pose an unacceptable risk in that organization's environment, or the risk may be forced upon the organization by business requirements. This may seem silly in the context of a security discussion, but in the real-world security concerns frequently fall prey to business justifications.

Vulnerability scanners have been known to take down the target system. Some IP implementations are not robust enough to handle many simultaneous connections, or IP packets with unusual flag combinations. The traffic generated by an aggressive port scan, for example, can sometimes crash a machine.

Finally, network vulnerability scanners tend to contain a huge amount of vulnerability data. If anyone ever breaks into the scanner system, compromise of most other machines on the network can become child's play. Protect the scanner to prevent unauthorized use of scanning data.

Host Vulnerability Scanner

A host vulnerability scanner differs from a network vulnerability scanner in that it is confined entirely to the local operating system. A network vulnerability scanner requires the target machine be accessible from the network in order for it to operate; a host vulnerability scanner does not.

Strengths

Host vulnerability scanners tend to be much more tuned and accurate for a given operating system. They can frequently tell the user which patches to apply to fix identified vulnerabilities, while network scanners sometimes only provide general guidelines. When considering which product to purchase, look at sample reports for your specific operating systems to determine how much information is contained in the reports. The depth and accuracy of reporting should be a selection criterion.

Host vulnerability scanners do not consume network bandwidth when they run. All processing is restricted to the local host system.

Host vulnerability scanners are not as likely as network scanners to cause the IP stack on the target system to hang. Some operating systems have weak or poorly implemented IP stacks associated with their network interfaces; sending a high volume of traffic (as a port scanner would do) or unusual TCP header flags may cause the interface to hang, which would necessitate a reboot.

Host vulnerability scanners are less likely to be used against you by a successful intruder. A hacker who breaks a system and finds a network vulnerability scanner, or reports from such a scanner, is likely to use the tool or the reports to attack other systems within your organization. A host based tool provides much less useful information for extending an attack; i.e., it is better compartmentalized than a network based tool.

Weaknesses

Host vulnerability scanners are, again, signature based. They look for known-dangerous system configurations and report on a cookbook approach to mitigating those particular threats. Local system procedures and operating requirements may require flexibility in finding and applying solutions to any given vulnerability.

Installing host vulnerability scanners requires the cooperation of system administrators.

Since the software usually runs with privilege, the system administrator for each machine should agree to the purpose and configuration of the tool. In many organizations, this can be a difficult coordination task.

As with any host-based system, attackers can modify the vulnerability scanner so it does not report on the vulnerabilities the attackers wish to exploit. There is an important corollary here—the vulnerability scanner cannot protect a system that was compromised when the scanner was installed.

Questions

Q.1. Define Intrusion Detection System and give the efficiency of Intrusion Detection System?

Q.2. What is IDS and what are the types of IDS, explain any one?

Q.3. Write a short notes of the following:

   (i) Network Vulnerability Scanner

  (ii) File Integrity Checker

 (iii) Network Based IDS

SECURITY POLICIES

The Information Security Policy establishes requirements to ensure that information security policies remain current as business needs evolve and technology changes. This policy must be published and communicated to employees and relevant external parties.

The Information Security Policy contains operational policies, standards, guidelines and metrics intended to establish minimum requirements for the secure delivery of government services. Secure service delivery requires the assurance of confidentiality, integrity, availability and privacy of government information assets through:

- Management and business processes that include and enable security processes.
- Ongoing personnel awareness of security issues.
- Physical security requirements for information systems.
- Governance processes for information technology.
- Reporting information security events and weaknesses.
- Creating and maintaining business continuity plans; and.
- Monitoring for compliance.

Need for Information Security Policies

The essence of security policy is to establish standards and guidelines for accessing your corporate information and application programs. Typically, organizations start with informal and undocumented security policies and procedures; but as your enterprise grows and your workforce becomes more mobile and diverse, it becomes especially important — even necessary — for your security policies to be documented in writing.

1. This information security policy provides management direction and support for information security across the organization, in both electronic and hard copy.

2. To determine the appropriate levels of security measures applied to information systems, a process of risk assessment is carried out for each system to identify the probability and impact of security failures.

3. To avoid any misunderstanding between the employee and employer.

4. To avoid any misunderstanding about distribution of work.

5. To avoid the misunderstanding about the distribution of IT assets between the employee and contractors.

6. To avoid any contradiction.

7. To provide the strict guideline for security of it assets.

8. To provide the strict guideline for protecting the information in IT environment.

9. It provides the guidelines necessary in determining the proper configuration of systems and a bar against which you can measure the effectiveness of your security efforts.

10. Provide a safe and secure information systems working environment for staff, students and any other authorized users.

WWW Policy

The World Wide Web is an important communication medium, and its use as a means of supporting and fulfilling the mission and official work of any organization.

The software provided to the employees for business can be used for any profit outside business:

Copyrights for documents and software

- The documents license govern documents such as technical reports.
- The software license govern distribution of w3c.
- In community and business groups, draft specifications are governed by w3c contributors.

Tradearks

- W3C trademarks governed by trademarks licenses. There are some additional policies for some logos such as w3c logos usage policies.

Patent Policies

- Patent policy enable continued innovation and wide spread adoption of web standards developed by w3c.

Privacy Policy

- The www policies set expectations about, how w3c will make use of information gathered during the course of your interactions with our websites.

Email Security Policy

Email is the electronic equivalent of a postcard. Because of this, it requires special policy considerations. From archiving to content guidelines, organizations have much to consider when writing email policies.

Rules for Using Email

General Rule for using email

1. Email should demonstrate the same respect thy gives to verbal communications.
2. Email should check thy spelling, thy grammar, and read thine own message thrice before thou send it.
3. Email should not forward any chain letter.
4. Email should not transmit unsolicited mass email (spam) unto anyone.
5. Email should not send messages that are hateful, harassing, or threatening unto fellow users.
6. Email should not send any message that supports illegal or unethical activities.
7. Email should remember thin email is the electronic equivalent of a post card and shalt not be used to transmit sensitive information.
8. Email should not use thin email broadcasting facilities except for making appropriate announcements.
9. Email should keep thy personal email use to a minimum.
10. Email should keep thy policies and procedures sacred and help administrators protect them from abusers.

Questions

Q.1. Define Security Policy and what are the needs of Information Security Policies?

Q.2. What is WWW policy, explain it with examples?

Q.2. What is E-Mail policy and what are the rules of using E-Mail?

Q.3. Write a short notes of the following:

    (*i*)   Trademark

    (*ii*)   Patent Policy

    (*iii*)   Copyrights for documents and software

Chapter 13

CYBER LAW

Cyber Law

Cyber Law is the law related to cyber space and governing cyber space. Cyber space is a very wide term and includes computers, networks, software, data storage devices (such as hard disks, USB disks etc), the Internet, websites, emails and even electronic devices such as mobile phones, ATM machines etc.

Cyber law encompasses laws relating to:

1. Cyber Crimes
2. Electronic and Digital Signatures
3. Intellectual Property
4. Data Protection and Privacy

1. **Cyber crimes** are unlawful acts where the computer is used either as a tool or a target or both. The enormous growth in electronic commerce (e-commerce) and online share trading has led to a phenomenal spurt in incidents of cyber crime.

2. **Electronic signatures** are used to authenticate electronic records. Digital signatures are one type of electronic signature. Digital signatures satisfy three major legal requirements – signer authentication, message authentication and message integrity.

3. Intellectual property is refers to creations of the human mind e.g. a story, a song, a painting, a design etc. The facets of **intellectual property** that relate to cyber space are covered by cyber law.

These includes:

- **Copyright Law** in relation to computer software, computer source code, websites, cell phone content etc.

- **Software and Source Code Licenses**
- **Trademark Law** with relation to domain names, meta tags, mirroring, framing, linking etc.
- **Semiconductor Law** which relates to the protection of semiconductor integrated circuits design and layouts.
- **Patent law** in relation to computer hardware and software.

Need for Cyber Law

There are various reasons why it is extremely difficult for conventional law to cope with cyberspace. Some of these are discussed below.

1. Cyberspace is an intangible dimension that is impossible to govern and regulate using conventional law.

2. Cyberspace has complete disrespect for jurisdictional boundaries. A person in India could break into a bank's electronic vault hosted on a computer in USA and transfer millions of Rupees to another bank in Switzerland, all within minutes. All he would need is a laptop computer and a cell phone.

3. Cyberspace handles gigantic traffic volumes every second. Billions of emails are crisscrossing the globe even as we read this, millions of websites are being accessed every minute and billions of dollars are electronically transferred around the world by banks every day.

4. Cyberspace is absolutely open to participation by all.

5. Cyberspace offers enormous potential for anonymity to its members. Readily available encryption software and steganographic tools that seamlessly hide information within image and sound files ensure the confidentiality of information exchanged between cyber-citizens.

6. Cyberspace offers never-seen-before economic efficiency. Billions of dollars worth of software can be traded over the Internet without the need for any government licenses, shipping and handling charges and without paying any customs duty.

7. Electronic information has become the main object of cyber crime. It is characterized by extreme mobility, which exceeds by far the mobility of persons, goods or other services. International computer networks can transfer huge amounts of data around the globe in a matter of seconds.

8. A software source code worth cores of rupees or a movie can be pirated across the globe within hours of their release.

Advantage of Cyber Laws

1. The IT Act 2000 attempts to change outdated laws and provides ways to deal with cyber crimes.

2. There is a need such laws so that people can perform purchase transactions over the Net through credit cards without fear of misuse.

3. The Act offers the much needed legal framework so that information is not denied legal effect.

4. In view of the growth in transactions and communications carried out through electronic records.

5. The Act had also proposed a legal framework for the authentication and origin of electronic records/ communications through digital signature.

6. Companies shall now be able to carry out electronic commerce using the legal infrastructure provided by the Act.

7. The Act throws open the doors for the entry of corporate companies in the business of being Certifying Authorities for issuing Digital Signatures Certificates.

8. The Act now allows Government to issue notification on the web thus heralding with any office.

COPYRIGHT ACT

Short title-

This Act may be called 1he Copyright (Amendment) Aa, 2012. Short title and (1) It shall come into force on such date as the Central Government may, by notification in the Official Gazette, appoint.

CHAPTER I Preliminary

Sec.1. Short title, extent and commencement. –

(1) This Act may be called the Copyright Act, 1957.

(2) It extends to the whole of India.

(3) It shall come into force on such date2 as the Central Government may, by notification in the Official Gazette, appoint.

Sec.2. Interpretation. –

In this Act, unless the context otherwise requires:

(*a*) **"adaptation" means:**

   (*i*)   in relation to a dramatic work, the conversion of the work into a non-dramatic work;

  (*ii*)   in relation to a literary work or an artistic work, the conversion of the work into a dramatic work by way of performance in public or otherwise;

 (*iii*)   in relation to a literary or dramatic work, any abridgement of the work or any version of the work in which the story or action is conveyed wholly or mainly by means of pictures in a form suitable for reproduction in a book, or in a newspaper, magazine or similar periodical.

  (*iv*)   in relation to a musical work, any arrangement or transcription of the work.

   (*v*)   in relation to any work, any use of such work involving its re-arrangement or iteration.

(*b*) **"work of architecture" means any building or structure having an artistic character or**

design, or any model for such building or structure.

(*c*) **"artistic work" means:**

  (*i*)   a painting, a sculpture, a drawing (including a diagram, map, chart or plan), an   engraving or a photograph, whether or not any such work possesses artistic quality.

  (*ii*)   work of architecture.

(*d*) **"author' means:**

  (*i*)   in relation to a literary or dramatic work, the author of the work.

  (*ii*)   in relation to a musical work, the composer;

  (*iii*)   in relation to an artistic work other than a photograph, the artist;

(*e*) "calendar year' means the year commencing on the 1st day of January.

(*f*) "cinematograph film" means any work of visual recording on any medium produced through a process from which a moving image may be produced by any means and includes a sound recording accompanying such visual recording and "cinematograph" shall be construed as including any work produced by any process analogous to cinematography including video films.

(*g*) "delivery", in relation to a lecture, includes delivery by means of any mechanical instrument or broadcast.

(*h*) "dramatic work" includes any piece for recitation, choreographic work or entertainment in dumb show, the scenic arrangement or acting form of which is fixed in writing or otherwise but does not include a cinematograph film.

  (*i*)   "engravings" include etchings, lithographs, wood-cuts, prints and other similar works, not being photographs.

  (j)   "exclusive license" means a license which confers on the licensee or on the licensee and persons authorized by him, to the exclusion of all other persons (including the owner of the copyright), any right comprised in the copyright in a work, and "exclusive licensee" shall be construed accordingly.

(*k*) "Government work" means a work which is made or published by or under the direction or control of-

  (*i*)   the Government or any department of the Government;

  (*ii*)   any Legislature in India;

(*m*) "infringing copy means:

  (*i*)   in relation to a literary, dramatic, musical or artistic work, a reproduction thereof otherwise than in the form of a cinematographic film.

  (*ii*)   in relation to a cinematographic film, a copy of the film made on any medium by any means

(*n*) "lecture" includes address, speech and sermon;

(*o*) "literary work" includes computer programmers, tables and compilations including computer "literary data bases.

(*p*) "musical work" means a work consisting of music and includes any graphical notation of such

work but does not include any words or any action intended to be sung, spoken or performed with the music.

(*q*) "performance", in relation to performer's right, means any visual or acoustic presentation made live by one or more performers.

(*r*) "photograph" includes photo-lithograph and any work produced by any process analogous to photography but does not include any part of a cinematograph film.

(*s*) "plate" includes any stereotype or other plate, stone, block, mould, matrix, transfer, negative [duplicating equipment] or other device used or intended to be used for printing or reproducing copies of any work, and any matrix or other appliance by which 27 Sound recording for the acoustic presentation of the work are or are intended to be made;

(*t*) "prescribed" means prescribed by rules made under this Act.

(*u*) "reprography" means the making of copies of a work, by photo-copying or similar means;

(*v*) "work" means any of the following works, namely:-

 (*i*) a literary, dramatic, musical or artistic work;

 (*ii*) a cinematograph film;

(*w*) "work of joint authorship" means a work produced by the collaboration of two or more authors in which the contribution of one author is not distinct from the contribution of the other author or authors;

CHAPTER II Copyright Office and Copyright Board

Sec.9. Copyright Office –

(1) There shall be established for the purposes of this Act an office to be called the Copyright Office.

(2) The Copyright Office shall be under the immediate control of the Registrar of Copyrights who shall act under the superintendence and direction of the Central Government.

(3) There shall be a seal for the Copyright Office.

Sec.10. Registrar and Deputy Registrars of Copyrights . –

(1) The Central Government shall appoint a Registrar of Copyrights and may appoint one or more Deputy Registrars of Copyrights.

(2) A Deputy Registrar of Copyrights shall discharge under the superintendence and direction of the Registrar of Copyrights such functions of the Registrar under this Act as the Registrar may, from time to time, assign to him; and any reference in this Act to the Registrar of Copyrights shall include a reference to a Deputy Registrar of Copyrights when so discharging any such functions.

Sec.11. Copyright Board. –

(1) As soon as may be after the commencement of this Act, the Central Government shall constitute a Board to be called the Copyright Board which shall consist of a Chairman and not less than two or more than[fourteen] other members.

(2) The Chairman and other members of the Copyright Board shall hold office for such period and on such terms and conditions as may be prescribed.

(3) The Chairman of the Copyright Board shall be a person who is, or has been, a Judge of High Court or is qualified for appointment as a Judge of a High Court.

(4) The Registrar of Copyrights shall be the Secretary of the Copyright Board and shall perform such functions as may be prescribed.

Sec.12. Powers and procedure of Copyright Board. –

(1) The Copyright Board shall, subject to any rules that may be made under this Act, have power to regulate its own procedure, including the fixing of places and times of its sittings:

Provided that the Copyright Board shall ordinarily hear any proceeding instituted before it under this Act within the zone in which, at the time of the institution of the proceeding, the person instituting the proceeding actually and voluntarily resides or carries on business or personally works for gain.

Explanation.- In this sub-section "zone" means a zone specified in section 15 of the States

Reorganization Act, 1956.

(2) The Copyright Board may exercise and discharge its powers and functions through Benches constituted by the Chairman of the Copyright Board from amongst its members, each Bench consisting of not less than three members.

"Provided that, if the Chairman is of opinion that any matter of importance is required to be heard by a larger bench, he may refer the matter to a special bench consisting of five members."

(3) If there is a difference of opinion among the members of the Copyright Board or any Bench thereof in respect of any matter coming before it for decision under this Act, the opinion of the majority shall prevail:

Provided that where there is no such majority, the opinion of the Chairman shall prevail.

CHAPTER III Copyright

Sec.13. Works in which copyright subsists.-

(1) Subject to the provisions of this section and the other provisions of this Act, copyright shall subsist throughout India in the following classes of works, that is to say-

 (a)   original literary, dramatic, musical and artistic works;

(*b*)   cinematograph films; and

(*c*)   sound recordings

(2) Copyright shall not subsist in any work specified in sub-section (1), other than a work to which the provisions of section 40 or section 41 apply:

  (*i*)   in the case of a published work, the work is first published in India, or where the work is first published outside India, the author is at the date of such publication, or in a case where the author was dead at that date, was at the time of his death, a citizen of India.

  (*ii*)   in the case of an unpublished work other than a 43 [work of architecture] the author is at the date of the making of the work a citizen of India or domiciled in India.

Explanation- in the case of a work of joint authorship, the conditions conferring copyright specified in this sub-section shall be satisfied by all the authors of the work.

Sec.14. Meaning of copyright.-For the purposes of this Act, "copyright" means the exclusive right subject to the provisions of this Act, to do or authorize the doing of any of the following acts in respect of a work or any substantial part thereof, namely:-

(a) in the case of a literary, dramatic or musical work, not being a computer programme, -

  (*i*)   to reproduce the work in any material form including the storing of it in any medium   by electronic means;

  (*ii*)   to issue copies of the work to the public not being copies already in circulation;

  (*iii*)   to perform the work in public, or communicate it to the public;

  (*iv*)   to make any cinematograph film or sound recording in respect of the work;

  (*v*)   to make any translation of the work;

  (*vi*)   to make any adaptation of the work;

Sec.15. Special provision regarding copyright in designs registered or capable of being registered under the Designs Act,1911.-

(1) Copyright shall not subsist under this Act in any design which is registered under the Designs Act, 1911.

(2) Copyright in any design, which is capable of being registered under the Designs Act, 1911, but which has not been so registered, shall cease as soon as any article to which the design has been applied has been reproduced more than fifty times by an industrial process by the owner of the copyright or, with his license, by any other person.

Sec.16. No copyright except as provided in this Act.-

No person shall be entitled to copyright or any similar right in any work, whether published or unpublished, otherwise than under and in accordance with the provisions of this Act or any other law for the time being in force, but nothing in this section shall be constructed as abrogating any right or jurisdiction to restrain a breach of trust or confidence.

CHAPTER IV Ownership of Copyright and the Rights of the Owner

Sec.17. First owner of copyright.-

Subject to the provisions of this Act, the author of a work shall be the first owner of the copyright therein Provided that-

(*a*) in the case of a literary, dramatic or artistic work made by the author in the course of his employment by the proprietor of a newspaper, magazine or similar periodical under a contract of service or apprenticeship, for the purpose of publication in a newspaper, magazine or similar periodical, the said proprietor shall, in the absence of any agreement to the contrary, be the first owner of the copyright in the work in so far as the copyright relates to the publication of the work in any newspaper, magazine or similar periodical, or to the reproduction of the work for the purpose of its being so published, but in all other respects the author shall be the first owner of the copyright in the work.

(*b*) subject to the provisions of clause (a), in the case of a photograph taken, or a painting or portrait drawn, or an engraving or a cinematograph film made, for valuable consideration at the instance of any person, such person shall, in the absence of any agreement to the contrary, be the first owner of the copyright.

Sec.18. Assignment of copyright. –

(1) The owner of the copyright in an existing work or the prospective owner of the copyright in a future work may assign to any person the copyright either wholly or partially and either generally or subject to limitations and either for the whole term of the copyright or any part thereof:

Provided that in the case of the assignment of copyright in any future work, the assignment shall take effect only when the work comes into existence.

(2) Where the assignee of a copyright becomes entitled to any right comprised in the copyright, the assignee as respects the rights so assigned, and the assignor as respects the rights not assigned, shall be treated for the purposes of this Act as the owner of copyright and the provisions of this Act shall have effect accordingly.

(3) In this section, the expression "assignee" as respects the assignment of the copyright in any future work includes the legal representatives of the assignee, if the assignee dies before the work comes into existence.

Sec.19.Mode of assignment.-

(1) No assignment of the copyright in any work shall be valid unless it is in writing signed by the assignor or by his duly authorised agent.

(2) The assignment of copyright in any work shall identify such work, and shall specify the rights assigned and the duration and territorial extent of such assignment.

(3) The assignment of copyright in any work shall also specify the amount of royalty payable, if any, to the author or his legal heirs during the currency of the assignment and the assignment shall be subject to revision, extension or termination on terms mutually agreed upon by the parties.

(4) Where the assignee does not exercise the rights assigned to him under any of the other subsections of this section within a period of one year from the date of assignment, the assignment in respect of such rights shall be deemed to have lapsed after the expiry of the said period unless otherwise specified in the assignment.

(5) If the period of assignment is not stated, it shall be deemed to be five years from the date of assignment.

(6) If the territorial extent of assignment of the rights is not specified, it shall be presumed to extend within India.

Sec.19A. Disputes with respect to assignment of copyright.-

(1) If an assignee fails to make sufficient exercise of the rights assigned to him, and such failure is not attributable to any act or omission of the assignor, then, the Copyright Board may, on receipt of a complaint from the assignor and after holding such inquiry as it may deem necessary, revoke such assignment.

(2) If any dispute arises with respect to the assignment of any copyright the Copyright Board may, on receipt of a complaint from the aggrieved party and after holding such inquiry as it considers necessary, pass such order as it may deem fit including an order for the recovery of any royalty payable:

Provided that the Copyright Board shall not pass any order under this sub-section to revoke the assignment unless it is satisfied that the terms of assignment are harsh to the assignor in case the assignor is also the author :

Provided further that no order of revocation of assignment under this sub-section, be made within a period of five years from the date of such assignment.

Sec.20. Transmission of copyright in manuscript by testamentary disposition

Sec.21. Right of author to relinquish copyright.-

(1) The author of a work may relinquish all or any of the rights comprised in the copyright in the work by giving notice in the prescribed form to the Registrar of Copyrights and thereupon such rights shall, subject to the provisions of sub-section (3), cease to exist from the date of the notice.

(2) On receipt of a notice under sub-section (1), the Registrar of Copyrights shall cause it to be published in the Official Gazette and in such other manner as he may deem fit.

(3) The relinquishment of all or any of the rights comprised in the copyright in a work shall not affect any rights subsisting in favour of any person on the date of the notice referred to in sub-section (1).

CHAPTER V Term of Copyright

Sec.22. Term of copyright in published literary, dramatic, musical and artistic works.-

Except as otherwise hereinafter provided, copyright shall subsist in any literary, dramatic, musical or artistic work (other than a photograph) published within the lifetime of the author until [sixty] years from the beginning of the calendar year next following the year in which the author dies.

Explanation.- In this section the reference to the author shall, in the case of a work of joint authorship, be construed as a reference to the author who dies last.

Sec.23. Term of copyright in anonymous and pseudonymous works.-

(1) In the case of a literary, dramatic, musical or artistic work (other than a photograph), which is published anonymously or pseudonymously, copyright shall subsist until [sixty] years from the beginning of the calendar year next following the year in which the work is first published :

Provided that where the identity of the author is disclosed before the expiry of the said period, copyright shall subsist until [sixty] years from the beginning of the calendar year next following the year in which the author dies.

(2) In sub-section (1), references to the author shall, in the case of an anonymous work of joint authorship, be construed,-

(a) where the identity of one of the authors is disclosed, as references to that author;

(b) where the identity of more authors than one is disclosed, as references to the author who dies last from amongst such authors.

Sec.24. Term of copyright in the posthumous work.-

(1) In the case of a literary, dramatic or musical work or an engraving, in which copyright subsists at the date of the death of the author or, in the case of any such work of joint authorship, at or immediately before the date of the death of the author who dies last, but which, or any adaptation of which, has not been published before that date, copyright shall subsist until [sixty] years from the beginning of the calendar year next following the year in which the work is first published or, where an adaptation of the work is published in any earlier year, from the beginning of the calendar year next following that year.

(2) For the purposes of this section a literary, dramatic or musical work or an adaptation of any such work shall be deemed to have been published, if it has been performed in public or if any records made in respect of the work have been sold to the public or have been offered for sale to the public.

Sec.25. Term of copyright in photographs.- In the case of a photograph, copyright shall subsist until [sixty] years from the beginning of the calendar year next following the year in which the photograph is published.

Sec.26. Term of copyright in cinematograph films.-In the case of a cinematograph film, copyright shall subsist until [sixty] years from the beginning of the calendar year next following the year in which the film is published.

Sec.27. Term of copyright in records.-In the case of a [sound recording], copyright shall subsist until sixty years from the beginning of the calendar year next following the year in which the [sound recording] is published.

Sec.28. Term of copyright in Government work.- In the case of Government work, where Government is the first owner of the copyright therein, copyright shall subsist until 71[Sixty] years from the beginning of the calendar year next following the year in which the work is first published.

Sec.28A. Term of copyright in works of public undertakings.- In the case of a work, where a public undertaking is the first owner of the copyright therein, copyright shall until [sixty] years from the beginning of the calendar year next following the year in which the work is first published.

Sec.29. Term of copyright in works of international organizations.- In the case of a work of an international organization to which the provisions of section 41 apply, copyright shall subsist until [sixty] years from the beginning of the calendar year next following the year in which the work is first published.

CHAPTER VI LICENSES

Sec.30.Licenses by owners of copyright.- The owner of the copyright in any existing work or the prospective owner of the copyright in any future work may grant any interest in the right by license in writing signed by him or by his duly authorized agent:

Provided that in the case of a license relating to copyright in any future work, the license shall take effect only when the work comes into existence.

Explanation.- Where a person to whom a license relating to copyright in any future work is granted under this section dies before the work comes into existence, his legal representatives shall, in the absence of any provision to the contrary in the license, be entitled to the benefit of the license.

Sec. 30A. Application of sections 19and 19A.-The provisions of sections 19 and 19A shall, with any necessary adaptations and modifications, apply in relation to a license under section 30 as they apply in relation to assignment of copyright in a work.

Sec.31. Compulsory license in works withheld from public.-

(1) If at any time during the term of copyright in any Indian work which has been published or performed in public, a complaint is made to the Copyright Board that the owner of copyright in the work-

    (a) has refused to republish or allow the republication of the work or has refused to allow the performance in public of the work, and by reason of such refusal the work is withheld from the public.

(b) has refused to allow communication to the public by [broadcast], of such work or in the case of [sound recording] the work recorded in such [sound recording], on terms which the complainant considers reasonable; the Copyright Board, after giving to the owner of the copyright in the work a reasonable opportunity of being heard and after holding such inquiry as it may deem necessary, may, if it is satisfied that the grounds for such refusal are not reasonable, direct the Registrar of Copyrights to grant to the complainant a license to republish the work, perform the work in public or communicate the work to the public by [broadcast], as the case may be, subject to payment to the owner of the copyright of such compensation and subject to such other terms and conditions as the Copyright Board may determine; and thereupon the Registrar of Copyrights shall grant the license to the complainant in accordance with the directions of the Copyright Board, on payment of such fee as may be prescribed.

Explanation.- In this sub-section, the expression "Indian work' includes-

(*i*) an artistic work, the author of which is a citizen of India.

(*ii*) a cinematograph film or a record made or manufactured in India.

Sec.31A.Compulsory license in unpublished Indian works.-

(1) Where, in the case of an Indian work referred to in sub-clause (iii) of clause (a) of section 2, the author is dead or unknown or cannot be traced, or the owner of the copyright in such work cannot be found, any person may apply to the Copyright Board for a license to publish such work or a translation thereof in any language.

(2) Before making an application under sub-section (1), the applicant shall publish his proposal in one issue of a daily newspaper in the English language having circulation in the major part of the country and where the application is for the publication of a translation in any language, also in one issue of any daily newspaper in that language.

Sec.32.License to produce and publish translations-

(1) Any person may apply to the Copyright Board for a license to produce and publish a translation of a literary or dramatic work in any language 2[after a period of seven years from the first publication of the work].

(1A) Notwithstanding anything contained in sub-section (1), any person may apply to the Copyright Board for a license to produce and publish a translation, in printed or analogous forms of reproduction, of a literary or dramatic work, other than an Indian work, in any language in general use in India after a period of three years from the publication of such work, if such translation is required for the purposes of teaching, scholarship or research:

Provided that where such translation is in a language not in general use in any developed country, such application may be made after a period of one year from such publications.

(2) Every [application under this section] shall be made in such form as may be prescribed and shall state the proposed retail price of a copy of the translation of the work.

(3) Every applicant for a license under this section shall, along with his application, deposit with the Registrar of Copyrights such fee as may be prescribed.

Sec.32A.License to reproduce and publish works for certain purposes.-

(1) Where, after the expiration of the relevant period from the date of the first publication of an edition of a literary, scientific or artistic work,-

   (*a*) the copies of such edition are not made available in India.

   (*b*) such copies have not been put on sale in India for a period of six months to the general public in connection with systematic instructional activities at a price reasonably related to that normally charged in India for comparable works by the owner of the right of reproduction or by any person authorized by him in this behalf, any person may apply to the Copyright Board for a license to reproduce and publish such work in printed or analogous forms of reproduction at the price at which such edition is sold or a lower price for the purposes of systematic instructional activities.

(2) Every such application shall be made in such form as may be prescribed and shall state the proposed retail price of a copy of the work to be reproduced.

(3) Every applicant for a license under this section shall, along with his application, deposit with the Registrar of Copyrights such fee as may be prescribed.

Sec.32B. Termination of licenses issued under this chapter.-

(1) If, at any time after the granting of a license to produce and publish the translation of a work in any language under sub-section (1A) of section 32 (hereafter in this sub-section referred to as the licensed work), the owner of the copyright in the work or any person authorized by him publishes a translation of such work in the same language and which is substantially the same in content at a price reasonably related to the price normally charged in India for the translation of works of the same standard on the same or similar subject, the license so granted shall be terminated:

Provided that no such termination shall take effect until after the expiry of a period of three months from the date of service of a notice in the prescribed manner on the person holding such license by the owner of the right of translation intimating the publication of the translation as aforesaid:

Provided further that copies of the licensed work produced and published by the person holding such license before the termination of the license takes effect may continue to be sold or distributed until the copies already produced and published are exhausted.

(2) If, at any time after the granting of a license to produce and publish the reproduction or translation of any work under section 32A, the owner of the right of reproduction or any person authorized by him sells or distributes copies of such work or a translation thereof, as the case may be, in the same language and which is substantially the same in content at a price reasonably related to the price normally charged in India for work of the same standard on the same or similar subject, the license so granted shall be terminated.

CHAPTER VII Copyright Societies

Sec.33. Registration of Copyright Society.-

(1) No person or association of persons shall, after coming into force of the Copyright (Amendment) Act, 1994 commence or, carry on the business of issuing or granting licenses in respect of any work in which copyright subsists on respect or in respect of any other rights conferred by this Act except under or in accordance with the registration granted under sub-section (3):

Provided that owner of copyright shall, in his individual capacity, continue to have the right to grant licenses in respect of his own works consistent with his obligations as a member of the registered copyright society:

Provided further that the performing rights society functioning in accordance with the provisions of section 33 on the date immediately before the coming into force of the Copyright (Amendment) Act, 1994 shall be deemed to be a copyright society for the purposes of this Chapter and every such society shall get itself registered within a period of one year from the date of commencement of the Copyright (Amendment) Act, 1994.

(2) Any association of persons who fulfils such conditions as may be prescribed may apply for permission to do the business specified in sub-section (1) to the Registrar of Copyrights who shall submit the application to the Central Government.

(3) The Central Government may, having regard to the interests of the authors and other owners of rights under this Act, the interest and convenience of the public and in particular of the groups of persons who are most likely to seek licenses in respect of the relevant rights and the ability and professional competence of the applicants, register such association of persons as a copyright society subject to such conditions as may be prescribed.

Sec.34. Administration of rights of owner by copyright society.-

(1) Subject to such conditions as may be prescribed-

(*a*) a copyright society may accept from an owner of rights exclusive authorization to administer any right in any work by issue of licenses or collection of license fees.

(*b*) an owner of rights shall have the right to withdraw such authorization without prejudice to the rights of the copyright society under any contract.

(2) It shall be competent for a copyright society to enter into agreement with any foreign society or organization administering rights corresponding to rights under this Act, to entrust to such foreign society or organization the administration in any foreign country of rights administered by the said copyright society in India, or for administering in India the rights administered in a foreign country by such foreign society or organization:

Provided that no such society or organization shall permit any discrimination in regard to the terms of license or the distribution of fees collected between rights in Indian and other works.

(3) Subject to such conditions as may be prescribed, a copyright society may-

    (*i*) issue licenses under section 30 in respect of any rights under this Act;

    (*ii*) collect fees in pursuance of such licenses;

    (*iii*) distribute such fees among owners of rights after making deductions for its own expenses.

Sec.34A.Payment of remuneration by copyright society.-

(1) If the Central Government is of the opinion that a copyright society for a class of work is generally administering the rights of the owners of rights in such work throughout India, it shall appoint that society for the purpose of this section.

(2) The copyright society shall, subject to such rules as may be made in this behalf, frame a scheme for determining the quantum of remuneration payable to individual copyright owners having regard to the number of copies of the work in circulation:

Provided that such scheme shall restrict payment to the owners of rights whose works have attained a level of circulation which the copyright society considers reasonable.

Sec.35. Control over the copyright society by the owner of rights.-

(1) Every copyright society shall be subject to the collective control of the owners of rights under this Act whose rights it administers (not being owners of rights under this Act administered by a foreign society or organization referred to in sub-section (2) of section (34) and shall, in such manner as may be prescribed,-

    (*a*) obtain the approval of such owners of rights for its procedures of collection and distribution of fees.

    (*b*) obtain their approval for the utilization of any amounts collected as fees for any purpose other than distribution to the owner of rights.

    (*c*) provide to such owners regular, full and detailed information concerning all its activities, in relation to the administration of their rights.

(2) All fees distributed among the owners of rights shall, as far as may be, be distributed in proportion to the actual use of their works.

Sec.36.Submission of returns and reports.-

(1) Every copyright society shall submit to the Registrar of Copyrights such returns as may be prescribed.

(2) Any officer duly authorized by the Central Government in this behalf may call for any report and also call for any records of any copyright society for the purpose of satisfying himself that the fees collected by the society in respect of rights administered by it are being utilized or distributed in accordance with the provisions of this Act.

Sec.36A.Rights and liabilities of performing rights societies.-

Nothing in this Chapter shall affect any rights or liabilities in any work in connection with a performing rights society which had accrued or were incurred on or before the day prior to the commencement of the Copyright (Amendment) Act, 1994, or any legal proceedings in respect of any such rights or liabilities pending on that day."

CHAPTER VIII Rights of Broadcasting 92 Organization and of Performers

Sec.37.Broadcast reproduction right.-

(1) Every broadcasting organization shall have a special right to be known as "broadcast reproduction right" in respect of its broadcasts.

(2) The broadcast reproduction right shall subsist until twenty-five years from the beginning of the calendar year next following the year in which the broadcast is made.

(3) During the continuance of a broadcast reproduction right in relation to any broadcast, any person who, without the license of the owner of the right does any of the following acts of the broadcast or any substantial part thereof,-

(*a*) re-broadcasts the broadcast.

(*b*) causes the broadcast to be heard or seen by the public on payment of any charges;

(*c*) makes any sound recording or visual recording of the broadcast;

Sec.38. Performer's right-

(1) Where any performer appears or engages in any performance, he shall have a special right to be known as the "performer's right" in relation to such performance.

(2) The performer's right shall subsist until 96A fifty years from the beginning of the calendar year next following the year in which the performance is made.

(3) During the continuance of a performer's right in relation to any performance, any person who, without the consent of the performer, does any of the following acts in respect of the performance or any substantial part thereof, namely :-

(*a*) makes a sound recording or visual recording of the performance; or

(*b*) reproduces a sound recording or visual recording of the performance, which sound recording or visual recording was:

(*i*) made without the performer's consent.

(*ii*) made for purposes different from those for which the performer gave his consent

Sec.39. Acts not infringing broadcast reproduction right or performer's right. –

No broadcast reproduction right or performer's right shall be deemed to be infringed by-

(a) the making of any sound recording or visual recording for the private use of the person making such recording, or solely for purposes of *bona fide* teaching or research; or

(b) the use, consistent with fair dealing, of excerpts of a performance or of a broadcast in the reporting of current events or for *bona fide* review, teaching or research.

Sec.39 A. Other provisions applying to broadcast reproduction right and performer's right.-

Sections 18, 19, 30, 53, 55, 58, 64, 65 and 66 shall, with any necessary adaptations and modifications, apply in relation to the broadcast reproduction right in any broadcast and the performers' right in any performance as they apply in relation to copyright in a work :

Provided that where copyright or performer's right subsists in respect of any work or performance that has been broadcast, no license to reproduce such broadcast shall take effect without the consent of the owner of rights or performer, as the case maybe, or both of them.

CHAPTER IX International Copyright

Sec.40. Power to extend copyright to foreign works.—

The Central Government may, by order published in the Official Gazette, direct that all or any provisions of this Act shall apply-

(a) to work first published in any class territory outside India to which the order relates in like manner as if they were first published within India;

(b) to unpublished works, or any class thereof, the authors whereof were at the time of the making of the work, subjects or citizens of a foreign country to which the order relates, in like manner as if the authors were citizens of India;

(c) in respect of domicile in any territory outside India to which the order relates in like manner as if such domicile were in India;

Sec.41. Provisions as to works of certain international organizations. –

(1) Where-

(*a*) any work is made or first published by or under the direction or control of any organization to which this section applies,

(*b*) there would, apart from this section, be no copyright in the work in India at the time of the making or, as the case may be, of the first publication thereof, and (*c*) either-

    (i)   the work is published as aforesaid in pursuance of an agreement in that behalf with the author, being an agreement which does not reserve to the author the copyright, if any, in the work.

    (ii)   under section 17 any copyright in the work would belong to the organization; there shall, by virtue of this section, be copyright in the work throughout India.

(2) Any organization to which this section applies which at the material time had not the legal capacity of a body corporate shall have and be deemed at all material times to have had the legal capacity of a body corporate for the purpose of holding, dealing with, and enforcing copyright and in connection with all legal proceedings relating to copyright.

(3) The organization to which this section applies are such organizations as the Central Government may, by order published in the Official Gazette, declare to be organizations of which one or more sovereign powers or the Government or Governments thereof are members to which it is expedient that this section shall apply.

Sec.42. Power to restrict rights in works of foreign authors first published in India. –

If it appears to the Central Government that a foreign country does not give or has not undertaken to give adequate protection to the works of Indian authors, the Central Government may, by order published in the Official Gazette, direct that such of the provisions of this Act as confer copyright on works first published in India shall not apply to works, published after the date specified in the order, the authors whereof are subjects or citizens of such foreign country and are not domiciled in India, and there upon those provisions shall not apply to such works.

Sec.43. Orders under this Chapter to be laid before Parliament.-

Every order made by the Central Government under this Chapter shall, as soon as may be after it is made, be laid before both Houses of Parliament and shall be subject to such modifications as Parliament may make during the session in which it is so laid or the session immediately following.

CHAPTER X Registration of Copyright

Sec.44. Register of Copyrights. -There shall be kept at the Copyright Office a register in the prescribed form to be called the Register of Copyrights in which may be entered the names or titles of works and the names and addresses of authors, publishers and owners of copyright and such other particulars as may be prescribed.

Sec.45. Entries in register of Copyrights. –

(1) The author or publisher of, or the owner of or other person interested in the copyright in, any work may make an application in the prescribed form accompanied by the prescribed fee to the Registrar of Copyrights for en2tering particulars of the work in the Register of Copyrights :

Provided that in respect of an artistic work which is used or is capable of being used in relation to any goods, the application shall include a statement to that effect and shall be accompanied by a certificate from the Registrar of Trade Marks referred to in section 4 of the Trade and Merchandise Marks Act, 1958, to the effect that no trade mark identical with or deceptively similar to such artistic work has been registered under that Act in the name of, or that no application has been made under that Act for such registration by, any person other than the applicant.]

(2) On receipt of an application in respect of any work under sub-section (1), the Registrar of Copyrights may, after holding such inquiry as he may deem fit, enter the particulars of the work in the Register of Copyrights.

Sec.46. Indexes. -There shall be also kept at the Copyright Office such indexes of the Register of Copyrights as may be prescribed.

Sec.47. Forms and inspection of register. -The Register of Copyrights and indexes thereof kept under this Act shall at all reasonable times be open to inspection, and any person shall be entitled to take copies of, or make extracts from, such register or indexes on payment of such fee and subject to such conditions as may be prescribed.

Se c.48. Register of Copyrights to be *prima facie* evidence of particulars entered therein.

The Register of Copyrights shall be prima facie evidence of the particulars entered therein and documents purporting to be copies of any entries therein, or extracts there from certified by the Registrar of Copyrights and sealed with the seal of the Copyright Office shall be admissible in evidence in all courts without further proof or production of the original.

Sec.49. Correction of entries in the Register of Copyrights –

The Registrar of Copyrights may, in the prescribed cases and subject to the prescribed conditions, amend or alter the Register of Copyrights by-

(a) correcting any error in any name, address or particulars;

(b) correcting any other error which may have arisen therein by accidental slip or omission.

Sec.50. Rectification of Register by Copyright Board.–

The Copyright Board, on application of the Registrar of Copyrights or of any person aggrieved, shall order the rectification of the Register of Copyrights by-

(a) the making of any entry wrongly omitted to be made in the register, or

(b) the expunging of any entry wrongly made in, or remaining on, the register, or

(c) the correction of any error or defect in the register.

Sec.50A. Entries in the Register of Copyrights ,etc, to be published.

Every entry made in the Register of Copyrights or the particulars of any work entered under section 45, the correction of every entry made in such register under section 49, and every rectification ordered under section 50, shall be published by the Registrar of Copyrights in the Official Gazette or in such other manner as he may deem fit.

CHAPTER XI Infringement of Copyright

Sec.51. When copyright infringed. –

21Copyright in a work shall be deemed to be infringed-

(*a*) when any person, without a license granted by the owner of the copyright or the Registrar of Copyrights under this Act or in contravention of the conditions of a license so granted or of any condition imposed by a competent authority under this Act-

(*i*) does anything, the exclusive right to do which is by this Act conferred upon the owner of the copyright,

(*ii*) permits for profit any place to be used for the communication of the work to the public where such communication constitutes an infringement of the copyright in the work, unless he was not aware and had no reasonable ground for believing that such communication to the public would be an infringement of copyright; or

(*b*) when any person-

(*i*) makes for sale or hire, or sells or lets for hire, or by way of trade displays or offers for sale or hire

or

(*ii*) distributes either for the purpose of trade or to such an extent as to affect prejudicially the owner the copyright,

(*iii*) by way of trade exhibits in public,

Sec.52. Certain acts not to be infringement of copyright. –

(1) The following acts shall not constitute an infringement of copyright, namely: a fair dealing with a literary, dramatic, musical or artistic work [not being a computer programme for the purposes of-

(*i*) private use, including research;

(*ii*) criticism or review, whether of that work or of any other work;

Sec.52A. Particulars to be included in records and video films.

(1) No person shall publish a [sound recording] in respect of any work unless the following particulars are displayed on the [sound recording] and on any container thereof, namely:-

(*a*) the name and address of the person who has made the [sound recording];

(*b*) the name and address of the owner of the copyright in such work; and

(*c*) the year of its first publication.

(2) No person shall publish a video film in respect of any work unless the following particulars are

displayed in the video film, when exhibited, and on the video cassette or other container thereof, namely :-

(*a*) if such work is a cinematograph film required to be certified for exhibition under the provisions of the Cinematograph Act, 1952, a copy of the certificate granted by the Broad of Film Certification under section 5A of that Act in respect of such work;

(*b*) the name and address of the person who has made the video film and a declaration by him that he has obtained the necessary license or consent from the owner of the copyright in such work for making such video film;

(*c*) the name and address of the owner of the copyright in such work.

Sec.52B. Accounts and Audit

Sec.53. Importation of infringing copies–

(1) The Registrar of Copyrights, on application by the owner of the copyright in any work or by his duly authorized agent and on payment of the prescribed fee, may, after making such inquiry as he deems fit, order that copies made out of India of the work which if made in India would infringe copyright shall not be imported.

(2) Subject to any rules made under this Act, the Registrar of Copyrights or any person authorized by him in this behalf may enter any ship, dock or premises where any such copies as are referred to in sub-section (1) may be found and may examine such copies.

Sec.53A. Resale share right in original copies.

(1) In the case of resale for a price exceeding ten thousand rupees, of the original copy of a painting, sculpture or drawing, or of the original manuscript of a literary or dramatic work or musical work, the author of such work if he was the first owner of rights under section 17 or his legal heirs shall, notwithstanding any assignment of copyright in such work, have a right to share in the resale-price of such original copy or manuscript in accordance with the revisions of this section:

Provided that such right shall cease to exist on the expiration of the term of copyright in the work.

(2) The share referred to in sub-section (1) shall be such as the Copyright Board may fix and the decision of the Copyright Board in this behalf shall be final.

CHAPTER XII Civil Remedies

Sec.54. Definition- For the purposes of this Chapter, unless the context otherwise requires, the expression "owner of copyright" shall include-

(a) an exclusive licensee;

(b) in the case of an anonymous or pseudonymous literary, dramatic, musical or artistic work, the publisher of the work, until the identity of the author or, in the case of an anonymous work of 1joint authorship, or a work of joint authorship published under names all of which are pseudonyms, the identity of any of the authors, is disclosed publicly by the author and the publisher or is otherwise established to the satisfaction of the Copyright Board by that author or his legal representatives.

Sec.55. Civil remedies for infringement of copyright –

(1) Where copyright in any work has been infringed, the owner of the copyright shall, except as otherwise provided by this Act, be entitled to all such remedies by way of injunction, damages, accounts and otherwise as are or may be conferred by law for the infringement of a right :

Provided that if the defendant proves that at the date of the infringement he was not aware and had no reasonable ground for believing that copyright subsisted in the work, the plaintiff shall not be entitled to any remedy other than an injunction in respect of the infringement and a decree for the whole or part of the profits made by the defendant by the sale of the infringing copies as the court may in the circumstances deem reasonable.

(2) Where, in the case of a literary, dramatic, musical or artistic work, a name purporting to be that of the author or the publisher, as the case may be, appears on copies of the work as published, or, in the case of an artistic work, appeared on the work when it was made, the person whose name so appears or appeared shall, in any proceeding in respect of infringement of copyright in such work, be presumed, unless the contrary is proved, to be the author or the publisher of the work, as the case may be.

(3) The costs of all parties in any proceedings in respect of the infringement of copyright shall be in the discretion of the court.

Sec.56. Protection of separate rights

Sec.57. Author's special rights.

(1) Independently of the author's copyright and even after the assignment either wholly or partially of the said copyright, the author of a work shall have the right-

(*a*)   to claim authorship of the work; and

(*b*)   to restrain or claim damages in respect of any distortion, mutilation, modification or other act in relation to the said work which is done before the expiration of the term of copyright if such distortion, mutilation, modification or other act would be prejudicial to his honor or reputation:

(2) The right conferred upon an author of a work by sub-section (1), other than the right to claim authorship of the work, may be exercised by the legal representatives of the author.

Sec.58. Rights of owner against persons possessing or dealing with infringing copies. –

All infringing copies of any work in which copyright subsists, and all plates used or intended to be used for the production of such infringing copies, shall be deemed to be the property of the owner of the copyright, who accordingly may take proceedings for the recovery of possession thereof or in respect of the conversion thereof :

Provided that the owner of the copyright shall not be entitled to any remedy in respect of the conversion of any infringing copies, if the opponent proves-

(*a*) that he was not aware and had no reasonable ground to believe that copyright subsisted in the work of which such copies are alleged to be infringing copies; or

(*b*) that he had reasonable grounds for believing that such copies or plates do not –involve infringement of the copyright in any work.

Sec.59. Restriction on remedies in the case of works of architecture. –

(1) Notwithstanding anything contained in [the Specific Relief Act, 1963], where the construction of a building or other structure which infringes or which, if completed, would infringe the copyright in some other work has been commenced, the owner of the copyright shall not be entitled to obtain an injunction to restrain the construction of such building or structure or to order its demolition.

(2) Nothing in section 58 shall apply in respect of the construction of a building or other structure which infringes or which, if completed, would infringe the copyright in some other work.

Sec.60. Remedy in the case of groundless threat of legal proceedings. –

Where any person claiming to be the owner of copyright in any work, by circulars, advertisements or otherwise, threatens any other person with any legal proceedings or liability in respect of an alleged infringement of the copyright, any person aggrieved thereby may, notwithstanding anything contained 124[in section 34 of the Specific Relief Act, 1963] institute a declaratory suit that the alleged infringement to which the threats related was not in fact an infringement of any legal rights of the person making such threats and may in any such suit-

(a) obtain an injunction against the continuance of such threats; and

(b) recover such damages, if any, as he has sustained by reason of such threats.

Sec.61. Owners of copyright to be party to the proceeding. –

(1) In every civil suit or other proceeding regarding infringement of copyright instituted by an exclusive licensee, the owner of the copyright shall, unless the court otherwise directs, be made a defendant and where such owner is made a defendant, he shall have the right to dispute the claim of the exclusive licensee.

(2) Where any civil suit or other proceeding regarding infringement of copyright instituted by an exclusive licensee is successful, no fresh suit or other proceeding in respect of the same cause of action shall lie at the instance of the owner of the copyright.

Sec.62. Jurisdiction of court over matters arising under this Chapter–

(1) Every suit or other civil proceeding arising under this Chapter in respect of the infringement of copyright in any work or the infringement of any other right conferred by this Act shall be instituted in the district court having jurisdiction.

(2) For the purpose of sub-section (1), and "district court having jurisdiction" shall, notwithstanding anything contained in the Code of Civil Procedure, 1908, or any other law for the time being in force, include a district court within the local limits of whose jurisdiction, at the time of the

institution of the suit or other proceeding, the person instituting the suit or other proceeding or, where there are more than one such persons, any of them actually and voluntarily resides or carries on business or personally works for gain.

CHAPTER XIII Offences

Sec.63. Offence of infringement of copyright or other rights conferred by this Act

Any person who knowingly infringes or abets the infringement of-

(a) the copyright in a work, or

(b) any other right conferred by this Act, 125[except the right conferred by section 53A]

Explanation.-Construction of a building or other structure which infringes or which, if completed, would infringe the copyright in some other work shall not be an offence under this section.

Sec.63A. Enhanced penalty on second and subsequent convictions

Sec.63B. Knowing use of infringing copy of computer programme to be an offence

Sec.64. Power of police to seize infringing copies –

(1) Any police officer, not below the rank of a sub-inspector, may, if he is satisfied that an offence under section 63 in respect of the infringement of copyright in any work has been, is being, or is likely to be, committed, seize without warrant, all copies of the work, and all plates used for the purpose of making infringing copies of the work, wherever found, and all copies and plates so seized shall, as soon as practicable, be produced before a Magistrate.]

(2) Any person having an interest in any copies of a work 132[or plates] seized under sub-section (1) may, within fifteen days of such seizure, make an application to the Magistrate for such copied. Or being restored to him and the Magistrate, after hearing the applicant and the complainant and making such further inquiry as may be necessary, shall make such order on the application as he may deem fit.

Sec.65. Possession of plates for purpose of making infringing copies

Sec.66. Disposal of infringing copies or plates for purpose of making infringing copies

Sec.67. Penalty for making false entries in register, etc., for producing or tendering false entries -

Any person who-

(*a*) makes or causes to be made a false entry in the Register of Copyrights kept under this Act.

(*b*) makes or causes to be made a writing falsely purporting to be a copy of any entry in such register,

(*c*) produces or tenders or causes to be produced or tendered as evidence any such entry or writing, knowing the same to be false, shall be punishable with imprisonment which may extend to one year, or with fine, or with both.

Sec.68.　Penalty for making false statements for the purpose of deceiving or influencing any authority or officer.

Any person who, -

(*a*)　with a view to deceiving any authority or officer in the execution provisions of this Act,

(*b*)　with a view to procuring or influencing the doing or omission of anything relation to this Act or any matter there under,

Sec.68A. Penalty for contravention of section 52A

Sec.69.　Offences by companies. –

(1)　Where any offence under this Act has been committed by a company, every person who at the time the offence was committed was in charge of, and was responsible to the company for, the conduct of the business of the company, as well as the company shall be deemed to be guilty of such offence and shall be liable to be proceeded against and punished accordingly:

(2)　Notwithstanding anything contained in sub-section (1), where an offence under this Act has been committed by a company, and it is proved that the offence was committed with the consent or connivance of, or is attributable to any negligence on the part of, any director, manager, secretary or other officer of the company, such director, manager, secretary or other officer shall also be deemed to be guilty of that offence and shall be liable to be proceeded against and punished accordingly.

　Explanation.- For the purposes of this section-

(a)　"company" means any body corporate and includes a firm or other association of persons;

(b)　"director" in relation to a firm means a partner in the firm.

　Sec.70. Cognizance of offences- No court inferior to that of 137a Metropolitan Magistrate or a Judicial Magistrate of the first class] shall try any offence under this Act.

CHAPTER XIV Appeals

Sec.71. Appeals against certain orders of Magistrate. –

Any person aggrieved by an order made under sub-section (2) of section 64 or section 66 may, within thirty days of the date of such order, appeal to the court to which appeals from the court making the order ordinarily lie, and such appellate court may direct that execution of the order be stayed pending disposal of the appeal.

Sec.72. Appeals against orders of Registrar of Copyrights and Copyright Board. –

(1)　Any person aggrieved by any final decision or order of the Registrar of Copyrights may, within three months from the date of the order or decision, appeal to the Copyright Board.

(2) Any person aggrieved by any final decision or order of the Copyright Board, not being a decision or order made in an appeal under sub-section (1), may, within three months from the date of such decision or order, appeal to the High Court within whose jurisdiction the appellant actually and voluntarily resides or carries on business or personally works for gain; Provided that no such appeal shall lie against a decision of the Copyright Board under section 6.

(3) In calculating the period of three months provided for an appeal under this section, the time taken in granting a certified copy of the order or record of the decision appealed against shall be excluded.

Sec.73. Procedure for appeals–

The High Court may make rules consistent with this Act as to the procedure to be followed in respect of appeals made to it under section 72.

CHAPTER XV Miscellaneous

Sec.74. Registrar of Copyrights and Copyright Board to possess certain powers of civil courts. -

The Registrar of Copyrights and the Copyright Board shall have the powers of a civil court when trying a suit under the Code of Civil Procedure, 1908, in respect of the following matters, namely :-

(a) summoning and enforcing the attendance of any person and examining him on oath;

(b) requiring the discovery and production of any document;(c) receiving evidence on affidavits;

(d) issuing commissions for the examination of witnesses or documents;

(e) requisitioning any public record or copy thereof from any court or office;

(f) any other matter which may be prescribed.

Explanation.- For the purpose of enforcing the attendance of witnesses, the local limits of the jurisdiction of the Registrar of Copyrights or the Copyright Board, as the case may be, shall be limits of the territory of India.

Sec.75. Orders for payment of money passed by Registrar of Copyrights and Copyright Board to be executable as a decree

Sec.76. Protection of action taken in good faith

Sec.77. Certain persons to be public servants

Sec.78. Power to make rules

(1) The Central Government may, by notification in the Official Gazette, make rules for carrying out the purposes of this Act.

(2) In particular, and without prejudice to the generality of the foregoing power, the Central

Government may make rules to provide for all or any of the following matters, namely:-

  (a) the term of office and conditions of service of the Chairman and other members of the Copyright Board;

  (b) the form of complaints and applications to be made, and the licenses to be granted, under this Act;

Sec.79. Repeals, savings and transitional provisions

THE PATENTS ACT, 1970

CHAPTER I PRELIMINARY

  (1) This Act may be called the Patents Act, 1970.

  (2) It extends to the whole of India.

  (3) It shall come into force on such date as the Central Government may, by notification in the Official Gazette, appoint:

Provided that different dates may be appointed for different provisions of this Act, and any reference in any such provision to the commencement of this Act shall be construed as a reference to the coming into force of that provision.

2. Definitions and interpretation.—

  (1) In this Act, unless the context otherwise requires,—

  (*a*) "Appellate Board" means the Appellate Board referred to in section 116;

  (ab) "assignee" includes an assignee of the assignee and the legal representative of a deceased assignee and references to the assignee of any person include references to the assignee of the legal representative or assignee of that person;

  (aba) "Budapest Treaty" means the Budapest Treaty on the International Recognition of the Deposit of Micro-organisms for the purposes of Patent Procedure done at Budapest on 28th day of April, 1977, as amended and modified from time to time;

  (ac) "capable of industrial application", in relation to an invention, means that the invention is capable of being made or used in an industry;

  (*b*) "Controller" means the Controller General of Patents, Designs and Trade Marks referred to in section 73;

  (*c*) "convention application" means an application for a patent made by virtue of section 135;

  (*d*) "convention country" means a country or a country which is member of a group of countries or a union of countries or an Intergovernmental organization referred to as a convention country in section 133;

(*e*) "district court" has the meaning assigned to that expression by the *Code* of Civil Procedure, 1908 (5 of 1908);

(*f*) "exclusive license" means a license from a patentee which confers on the licensee, on the licensee and persons authorised by him, to the exclusion of all other persons (including the patentee), any right in respect of the patented invention, and exclusive licensee shall be construed accordingly.

(*g*) Omitted by the *Patents (Amendment) Act,* 2005

(*h*) "Government undertaking" means any industrial undertaking carried on—

    (*i*) by a department of the Government.

    (*ii*) by a corporation established by a Central, Provincial or State Act, which is owned or controlled by the Government, or (iii) by a Government company as defined in section 617 of the Companies Act, 1956 (1 of 1956), or

    (*iv*) by an institution wholly or substantially financed by the Government;

(*i*) "High Court", in relation to a State or Union territory, means the High Court having territorial jurisdiction in that State or Union territory, as the case may be;

(*ia*) "international application" means an application for patent made in accordance with the Patent Cooperation Treaty;

(j)"invention" means a new product or process involving an inventive step and capable of industrial application;

(*ja*) "inventive step" means a feature of an invention that involves technical advance as compared to the existing knowledge or having economic significance or both and that makes the invention not obvious to a person skilled in the art;

(*k*) "legal representative" means a person who in law represents the estate of a deceased person;

(l) "new invention" means any invention or technology which has not been anticipated by publication in any document or used in the country or elsewhere in the world before the date of filing of patent application with complete specification, i.e., the subject matter has not fallen in public domain or that it does not form part of the state of the art;

(la) "Opposition Board" means an Opposition Board constituted under sub-section (3) of section 25;

(m) "patent" means a patent for any invention granted under this Act;

(n) "patent agent" means a person for the time being registered under this Act as a patent agent;

(o) "patented article" and "patented process" means respectively an article or process in respect of which a patent is in force;

(oa) "Patent Cooperation Treaty" means the Patent Cooperation Treaty done at Washington on the 19th day of June, 1970 as amended and modified from time to time;

(p) "patentee" means the person for the time being entered on the register as the grantee or proprietor of the patent;

(q) "patent of addition" means a patent granted in accordance with section 54;

(r) "patent office" means the patent office referred to in section 74;

(s) "person" includes the Government;

(t) "person interested" includes a person engaged in, or in promoting, research in the same field as that to which the invention relates;

(ta) "pharmaceutical substance" means any new entity involving one or more inventive steps;

(u) "prescribed" means,—

(A) in relation to proceedings before a High Court, prescribed by rules made by the High Court;

(B) in relation to proceedings before the Appellate Board, prescribed by rules made by the Appellate Board; and

(C) in other cases, prescribed by rules made under this Act;

(v) "prescribed manner" includes the payment of the prescribed fee;

(w) "priority date" has the meaning assigned to it by section 11;

(x) "register" means the register of patents referred to in section 67;

(y) "true and first inventor" does not include either the first importer of an invention into India, or a person to whom an invention is first communicated from outside India.

(2) In this Act, unless the context otherwise requires, any reference—

(a) to the Controller shall be construed as including a reference to any officer discharging the functions of the Controller in pursuance of section 73;

(b) to the patent office shall be construed as including a reference to any branch office of the patent office.

CHAPTER II INVENTIONS NOT PATENTABLE

Section 3. What are not inventions.—

The following are not inventions within the meaning of this Act,—

(a) an invention which is frivolous or which claims anything obviously contrary to well established natural laws;

(b) an invention the primary or intended use or commercial exploitation of which could be contrary public order or morality or which causes serious prejudice to human, animal or plant life or health or to the environment;

(c) the mere discovery of a scientific principle or the formulation of an abstract theory or discovery of any living thing or non-living substance occurring in nature;

(d) the mere discovery of a new form of a known substance which does not result in the enhancement of the known efficacy of that substance or the mere discovery of any new property or new use for a known substance or of the mere use of a known process, machine or apparatus unless such known process results in a new product or employs at least one new reactant.

Explanation.—For the purposes of this clause, salts, esters, ethers, polymorphs, metabolites, pure form, particle size, isomers, mixtures of isomers, complexes, combinations and other derivatives of known substance shall be considered to be the same substance, unless they differ significantly in properties with regard to efficacy;

(*e*) a substance obtained by a mere admixture resulting only in the aggregation of the properties of the components thereof or a process for producing such substance;

(*f*) the mere arrangement or re-arrangement or duplication of known devices each functioning independently of one another in a known way;

(*g*) Omitted by the *Patents (Amendment) Act,* 2002

(*h*) a method of agriculture or horticulture;

(*i*) any process for the medicinal, surgical, curative, prophylactic diagnostic, therapeutic or other treatment of human beings or any process for a similar treatment of animals to render them free of disease or to increase their economic value or that of their products.

(*j*) plants and animals in whole or any part thereof other than micro organisms but including seeds, varieties and species and essentially biological processes for production or propagation of plants and animals;

(*k*) a mathematical or business method or a computer programme *per se* or algorithms;

(*l*) a literary, dramatic, musical or artistic work or any other aesthetic creation whatsoever including cinematographic works and television productions;

(*m*) a mere scheme or rule or method of performing mental act or method of playing game;

(*n*) a presentation of information;

Section 4. Inventions relating to atomic energy not patentable.—

No patent shall be granted in respect of an invention relating to atomic energy falling within sub section (1) of section 20 of the Atomic Energy Act, 1962 (33 of 1962).

Section 5. Inventions where only methods or processes of manufacture patentable:

[Omitted by the *Patents (Amendment) Act,* 2005]

CHAPTER III APPLICATIONS FOR PATENTS

Section 6. Persons entitled to apply for patents—

(1) Subject to the provisions contained in section 134, an application for a patent for an invention may be made by any of the following persons, that is to say,—

(*a*) by any person claiming to be the true and first inventor of the invention;

(*b*)   by any person being the assignee of the person claiming to be the true and first inventor in respect of the right to make such an application;

(*c*)   by the legal representative of any deceased person who immediately before his death was entitled to make such an application.

Section 7. Form of application.—

(1)   Every application for a patent shall be for one invention only and shall be made in the prescribed form and filed in the patent office.

(2)   Where the application is made by virtue of an assignment of the right to apply for a patent for the invention, there shall be furnished with the application, or within such period as may be prescribed after the filing of the application, proof of the right to make the application.

(3)   Every application under this section shall state that the applicant is in possession of the invention and shall name the person claiming to be the true and first inventor; and where the person so claiming is not the applicant or one of the applicants, the application shall contain a declaration that the applicant believes the person so named to be the true and first inventor.

(4)   Every such application (not being a convention application or an application filed under the Patent Cooperation Treaty designating India) shall be accompanied by a provisional or a complete specification.

Section 10. Contents of specifications.—

(1)   Every specification, whether provisional of complete, shall describe the invention and shall begin with a title sufficiently indicating the subject-matter to which the invention relates.

(2)   Subject to any rules that may be made in this behalf under this Act, drawings may, and shall, if the Controller so requires, be supplied for the purposes of any specification, whether complete or provisional; and any drawings so supplied shall, unless the Controller otherwise directs be deemed to form part of the specification, and references in this Act to a specification shall be construed accordingly.

(3)   If, in any particular case, the Controller considers that an application should be further supplemented by a model or sample of anything illustrating the invention or alleged to constitute an invention, such model or sample as he may require shall be furnished before the application is found in order for grant of a patent, but such model or sample shall not be deemed to form part of the specification.

(4)   Every complete specification shall—

(*a*)   fully and particularly describe the invention and its operation or use and the method by which it is to be performed

(*b*)   disclose the best method of performing the invention which is known to the applicant and for which he is entitled to claim protection;

(*c*) end with a claim or claims defining the scope of the invention for which protection is claimed;

(*d*) be accompanied by an abstract to provide technical information on the invention:

Provided that—

(*i*) the Controller may amend the abstract for providing better information to third parties; and

(*ii*) if the applicant mentions a biological material in the specification which may not be described in such a way as to satisfy clauses (*a*) and (*b*), and if such material is not available to the public, the application shall be completed by depositing the material to an international depository authority under the Budapest Treaty and by fulfilling the following conditions, namely:—

(A) the deposit of the material shall be made not later than the date of filing the patent application in India and a reference thereof shall be made in the specification within the prescribed period;

(B) all the available characteristics of the material required for it to be correctly identified or indicated are included in the specification including the name, address of the depository institution and the date and number of the deposit of the material at the institution;

(C) access to the material is available in the depository institution only after the date of the application of patent in India or if a priority is claimed after the date of the priority;

(D) disclose the source and geographical origin of the biological material in the specification, when used in an invention.

(4A) In case of an international application designating' India, the title, description, drawings, abstract and claims filed with the application shall be taken as the complete specification for the purposes of this Act.

(5) The claim or claims of a complete specification shall relate to a single invention, or to a group of inventions linked so as to form a single inventive concept, shall be clear and succinct and shall be fairly based on the matter disclosed in the specification.

(6) A declaration as to the inventor ship of the invention shall, in such cases as may be prescribed, be furnished in the prescribed form with the complete specification or within such period as may be prescribed after the filing of that specification.

(7) Subject to the foregoing provisions of this section, a complete specification filed after a provisional specification may include claims in respect of developments of, or additions to, the invention which was described in the provisional specification, being developments or additions in respect of which the applicant would be entitled under the provisions of section 6 to make a separate application for a patent.

Section 11. Priority dates of claims of a complete specification

(1) There shall be a priority date for each claim of a complete specification.

(2) Where a complete specification is filed in pursuance of a single application accompanied by—

(*a*) a provisional specification;

(*b*)   a specification which is treated by virtue of a direction under subsection (3) of section 9 as a provisional specification, and the claim is fairly based on the matter disclosed in the specification referred to in clause (*a*) or clause (*b*), the priority date of that claim shall be the date of the filing of the relevant specification.

(3)   Where the complete specification is filed or proceeded with in pursuance of two or more applications accompanied by such specifications as are mentioned in sub-section (2) and the claim is fairly based on the matter disclosed—

(*a*)   in one of those specifications, the priority date of that claim shall be the date of the filing of the application accompanied by that specification;

(*b*)   partly in one and partly in another, the priority date of that claim shall be the date of the filing of the application accompanied by the specification of the later date.

(3A)   Where a complete specification based on a previously filed application in India has been filed within twelve months from the date of that application and the claim is fairly based on the matter disclosed in the previously filed application, the priority date of that claim shall be the date of the previously filed application in which the matter was first disclosed.

(4)   Where the complete specification has been filed in pursuance of a further application made by virtue of sub-section (1) of section 16 and the claim is fairly based on the matter disclosed in any of the earlier specifications, provisional or complete, as the case may be, the priority date of that claim shall be the date of the filing of that specification in which the matter was first disclosed.

(5)   Where, under the foregoing provisions of this section, any claim of a complete specification would, but for the provisions of this sub-section, have two or more priority dates, the priority date of that claim shall be the earlier or earliest of those dates.

(6)   In any case to which sub-sections (2), (3), (3A), (4) and (5) do not apply, the priority date of a claim shall, subject to the provisions of section 137, be the date of filing of the complete specification.

(7)   The reference to the date of the filing of the application or of the complete specification in this section shall, in cases where there has been a post-dating under section 9 or section 17 or, as the case may be, an ante-dating under section 16, be a reference to the date as so post-dated or ante-dated.

(8)   A claim in a complete specification of a patent shall not be invalid by reason only of—

(*a*)   the publication or use of the invention so far as claimed in that claim on or after the priority date of such claim; or

(*b*)   the grant of another patent which claims the invention, so far as claimed in the first mentioned claim, in a claim of the same or a later priority date.

CHAPTER IV PUBLICATION AND EXAMINATION OF APPLICATIONS

Sec.11A. Publication of applications

Sec.11B. Request for examination

Sec.12. Examination of application

Sec.13. Search for anticipation by previous publication and by prior claim.

Sec.14. Consideration of the report of examiner by Controller.

Sec.15. Power of Controller to refuse or require amended applications, etc., in certain case16. Power of Controller to make orders respecting division of application.

Sec.17. Power of Controller to make orders respecting dating of application.

Sec.18. Powers of Controller in cases of anticipation.

(1) Where it appears to the Controller that the invention so far as claimed in any claim of the complete specification has been anticipated in the manner referred to in clause (a) of sub section (1) or sub-section (2) of section 13, he may refuse the application unless the applicant—

   (*a*)   shows to the satisfaction of the Controller that the priority date of the claim of his complete specification is not later than the date on which the relevant document was published; or

   (*b*)   amends his complete specification to the satisfaction of the Controller.

(2) If it appears to the Controller that the invention is claimed in a claim of any other complete specification referred to in clause (b) of sub-section (1) of section 13, he may, subject to the provisions hereinafter contained, direct that a reference to that other specification shall be inserted by way of notice to the public in the applicant's complete specification unless within such time as may be prescribed,—

   (*a*)   the applicant shows to the satisfaction of the Controller that the priority date of his claim is not later than the priority date of the claim of the said other specification; or

   (*b*)   the complete specification is amended to the satisfaction of the Controller.

(3) If it appears to the Controller, as a result of an investigation under section 13 or otherwise,—

   (*a*)   that the invention so far as claimed in any claim of the applicant's complete specification has been claimed in any other complete specification referred to in clause (a) of sub-section (1) of section 13; and

   (*b*)   that such other complete specification was published on or after the priority date of the applicant's claim, then, unless it is shown to the satisfaction of the Controller that the priority date of the applicant's claim is not later than the priority date of the claim of that specification, the provisions of sub-section (2) shall apply thereto in the same manner as they apply to a specification published on or after the date of filing of the applicant's complete specification.

(4) Omitted by the *Patents (Amendment) Act,* 2005

Sec.19. Powers of Controller in case of potential infringement

Sec.20. Powers of Controller to make orders regarding substitution of applicants, etc

Sec.21. Time for putting application in order for grant.—(1) An application for a patent shall be deemed to have been abandoned unless, Within such period as may be prescribed, the applicant has complied with all the requirements imposed on him by or under this Act, whether in connection with the complete specification or otherwise in relation to the application from the date on which the first statement of objections to the application or complete specification or other documents related thereto is forwarded to the applicant by the Controller.

Explanation:- Where the application for a patent or any specification or, in the case of a convention application or an application filed under the Patent Cooperation Treaty designating India any document filed as part of the application has been returned to the applicant by the Controller in the course of the proceedings, the applicant shall not be deemed to have complied with such requirements unless and until he has re-filed it or the applicant proves to the satisfaction of the Controller that for the reasons beyond his control such document could not be re-filed.

(2) If at the expiration of the period as prescribed under sub section (1),—

(a)   an appeal to the High Court is pending in respect of the application for the patent for the main invention; or

(b)   in the case of an application for a patent of addition, an appeal to the High Court is pending in respect of either that application or the application for the main invention, the time within which the requirements of the Controller shall be complied with shall, on an application made by the applicant before the expiration of the period as prescribed under sub-section (1), be extended until such date as the High Court may determine.

(3) If the time within which the appeal mentioned in sub-section (2) may be instituted has not expired, the Controller may extend the period as prescribed under sub-section (1), to such further period as he may determine:

Provided that if an appeal has been filed during the said further period, and the High Court has granted any extension of time for complying with the requirements of the Controller, then the requirements may be complied with within the time granted by the Court.

Sec.22. Acceptance of complete specification.- [Omitted by the *Patents (Amendment) Act,* 2005]

Sec.23. Advertisement of acceptance of complete specification.- [Omitted by the *Patents (Amendment) Act,* 2005]

Sec.24. Effect of acceptance of complete specification.- [Omitted by the *Patents (Amendment) Act,* 2005]

CHAPTER V OPPOSITION PROCEEDINGS TO GRANT OF PATENTS

Sec.25. Opposition to the patent

Sec.26. In cases of "obtaining" Controller may treat the patent as the patent of opponent

Refusal to patent without opposition.—[Omitted by the *Patents (Amendment) Act,* 2005,]

Sec.28. Mention of inventor as such in patent

CHAPTER VI ANTICIPATION

CHAPTER VII PROVISIONS FOR SECRECY OF CERTAIN INVENTIONS

CHAPTER VIII GRANT OF PATENTS AND RIGHTS CONFERRED THEREBY

Sec.43. Grant of patents.—

(1) Where an application for a patent has been found to be in order for grant of the patent and either—

   (*a*) the application has not been refused by the Controller by virtue of any power vested in him by this Act; or

   (*b*) the application has not been found to be in contravention of any of the provisions of this Act, the patent shall be granted as expeditiously as possible to the applicant or, in the case of a joint application, to the applicants jointly, with the seal of the patent office and the date on which the patent is granted shall be entered in the register.

(2) On the grant of patent, the Controller shall publish the fact that the patent has been granted and thereupon the application, specification and other documents related thereto shall be open for public inspection.

Sec.44. Amendment of patent granted to deceased applicant

Sec.45. Date of patent.—

(1) Subject to the other provisions contained in this Act, every patent shall be dated as of the date on which the application for patent was filed.

(2) The date of every patent shall be entered in the register.

(3) Notwithstanding anything contained in this section, no suit or other proceeding shall be commenced or prosecuted in respect of an infringement committed before the date of publication of the application.

Sec.46. Form, extent and effect of patent.—

(1) Every patent shall be in the prescribed form and shall have effect throughout India.

(2) A patent shall be granted for one invention only:

Provided that it shall not be competent for any person in a suit or other proceeding to take any objection to a patent on the ground that it has been granted for more than one invention.

Sec.47. Grant of patents to be subject to certain conditions.—The grant of a patent under this Act shall be subject to the condition that—

(1) any machine, apparatus or other article in respect of which the patent is granted or any article made by using a process in respect of which the patent is granted, may be imported or made by or on behalf of the Government for the purpose merely of its own use;

(2) any process in respect of which the patent is granted may be used by or on behalf of the Government for the purpose merely of its own use;

(3) any machine, apparatus or other article in respect of which the patent is granted or any article made by the use of the process in respect of which the patent is granted, may be made or used, and any process in respect of which the patent is granted may be used, by any person, for the purpose merely of experiment or research including the imparting of instructions to pupils;

(4) in the case of a patent in respect of any medicine or drug, the medicine or drug may be imported by the Government for the purpose merely of its own use or for distribution in any dispensary, hospital or other medical institution maintained by or on behalf of the Government or any other dispensary, hospital or other medical institution which the Central Government may, having regard to the public service that such dispensary, hospital or medical institution renders, specify in this behalf by notification in the Official Gazette.

Sec.48. Rights of patentees.—Subject to the other provisions contained in this Act and the conditions specified in section 47, a patent granted under this Act shall confer upon the patentee—

(a) where the subject matter of the patent is a product, the exclusive right to prevent third parties, who do not have his consent, from the act of making, using, offering for sale, selling or importing for those purposes that product in India;

(b) where the subject matter of the patent is a process, the exclusive right to prevent third parties, who do not have his consent, from the act of using that process, and from the act of using, offering for sale, selling or importing for those purposes the product obtained directly by that process in India:

Sec.49. Patent rights not infringed when used on foreign vessels etc., temporarily or accidentally in India.—

(1) Where a vessel or aircraft registered in a foreign country or a land vehicle owned by a person ordinarily resident in such country comes into India (including the territorial waters thereof) temporarily or accidentally only, the rights conferred by a patent for an invention shall not be deemed to be infringed by the use of the invention—

(a) in the body of the vessel or in the machinery, tackle, apparatus or other accessories thereof, so far as the invention is used on board the vessel and for its actual needs only; or

(b) in the construction or working of the aircraft or land vehicle or of the accessories thereof, as the case may be.

(2) This section shall not extend to vessels, aircrafts or land vehicles owned by persons ordinarily resident in a foreign country the laws of which do not confer corresponding rights with respect to the use of inventions in vessels, aircraft or land vehicles owned by persons ordinarily resident in India while in the ports or within the territorial waters of that foreign country or otherwise within the jurisdiction of its courts.

Sec.50. Rights of co-owners of patents

Sec.51. Power of Controller to give directions to co-owners

(3) Before giving any directions in pursuance of an application under this section, the Controller shall give an opportunity to be heard—

(*a*) in the case of an application under sub-section (1) to the other person or persons registered as grantee or proprietor of the patent;

(*b*) in the case of an application under sub-section (2), to the person in default.

(*4*) No direction shall be given under this section so as to affect the mutual rights or obligations of trustees or of the legal representatives of a deceased person or of their rights or obligations as such, or which is inconsistent with the terms of any agreement between persons registered as grantee or proprietor of the patent.

Sec.52. Grant of patent to true and first inventor where it has been obtained by another in fraud of him

Sec.53. Term of patent.—

(1) Subject to the provisions of this Act, the term of every patent granted, after the commencement of the Patents (Amendment) Act, 2002, and the term of every patent which has not expired and has not ceased to have effect, on the date of such commencement, under this Act, shall be twenty years from the date of filing of the application for the patent.

Explanation.—For the purposes of this sub-section, the term of patent in case of International applications filed under the Patent Cooperation Treaty designating India, shall be twenty years from the international filing date accorded under the Patent Cooperation Treaty.

(2) A patent shall cease to have effect notwithstanding anything therein or in this Act on the expiration of the period prescribed for the payment of any renewal fee, if that fee is not paid within the prescribed period or within such extended period as may be prescribed.

(3) [Omitted by the *Patents (Amendment) Act, 2005*]

(4) Notwithstanding anything contained in any other law for the time being in force, on cessation of the patent right due to non-payment of renewal fee or on expiry of the term of patent, the subject matter covered by the said patent shall not be entitled to any protection.

CHAPTER XII SURRENDER AND REVOCATION OF PATENTS

Sec.63. Surrender of patents.—

(1) A patentee may, at any time by giving notice in the prescribed manner to the Controller, offer to surrender his patent.

(2) Where such an offer is made, the Controller shall publish the offer in the prescribed manner, and also notify every person other than the patentee whose name appears in the register as having an interest in the patent.

(3) Any person interested may, within the prescribed period after such publication, give notice to the Controller of opposition to the surrender, and where any such notice is given the Controller shall notify the patentee.

(4) If the Controller is satisfied after hearing the patentee and any opponent, if desirous of being heard, that the patent may properly be surrendered, he may accept the offer and, by order, revoke the patent.

Flashlig Sec.64. Revocation of patents.—(1) Subject to the provisions contained in this Act, a patent, whether granted before or after the commencement of this Act, may, be revoked on a petition of any person interested or of the Central Government by the Appellate Board or on a counter-claim in a suit for infringement of the patent by the High Court on any of the following grounds, that is to say—

(*a*) that the invention, so far as claimed in any claim of the complete specification, was claimed in a valid claim of earlier priority date contained in the complete specification of another patent granted in India;

(*a*) that the patent was granted on the application of a person not entitled under the provisions of this Act to apply therefor:

(*a*) that the patent was obtained wrongfully in contravention of the rights of the petitioner or any person under or through whom he claims;

(*d*) that the subject of any claim of the complete specification is not an invention within the meaning of this Act;

(*f*) that the invention so far as claimed in any claim of the complete specification is obvious or does not involve any inventive step, having regard to what was publicly known or publicly used in India or what was published in India or elsewhere before the priority date of the claim:

(*g*) that the invention, so far as claimed in any claim of the complete specification, is not useful;

(*h*) that the complete specification does not sufficiently and fairly describe the invention and the method by which it is to be performed, that is to say, that the description of the method or the instructions for the working of the invention as contained in the complete specification are not by themselves sufficient to enable a person in India possessing average skill in, and average knowledge of, the art to which the invention relates, to work the invention, or that it does not disclose the best method of performing it which was known to the applicant for the patent and for which he was entitled to claim protection;

(*i*) that the scope of any claim of the complete specification is not sufficiently and clearly defined or that any claim of the complete specification is not fairly based on the matter disclosed in the specification;

Sec.66. Revocation of patent in public interest.—Where the Central Government is of opinion that a patent or the mode in which it is exercised is mischievous to the State or generally prejudicial to the public, it may, after giving the patentee an opportunity to be heard, make a declaration to that effect in the Official Gazette and thereupon the patent shall be deemed to be revoked.

CHAPTER XIII REGISTER OF PATENTS

Sec. 67. Register of patents and particulars to be entered therein.—

(1) There shall be kept at the patent office a register of patents, wherein shall be entered—

    (*a*) the names and addresses of grantees of patents;

    (*b*) notifications of assignments, extension, and revocations of patents; and

    (*c*) particulars of such other matters affecting the validity or proprietorship of patents as may be prescribed.

(2) No notice of any trust, whether express, implied or constructive, shall be entered in the register, and the Controller shall not be affected by any such notice.

(3) Subject to the superintendence and directions of the Central Government, the register shall be kept under the control and management of the Controller.

(4) Notwithstanding anything contained in sub-section (1), it shall be lawful for the Controller to keep the register of patents or any part thereof in computer floppies, diskettes or any other electronic form subject to such safeguards as may be prescribed.

Sec.68. Assignments, etc., not to be Valid Unless in Writing and Duly Executed

Sec.69. Registration of Assignments, Transmissions

Sec.70. Power of Registered Grantee or Proprietor to Deal with patent-

Subject to the provisions contained in this Act relating to co-ownership of patents and subject also to any rights vested in any other person of which notice is entered in the register, the person or persons registered as grantee or proprietor of a patent shall have power to assign, grant licenses under, or otherwise deal with, the patent and to give effectual receipts for any consideration for any such assignment, license or dealing:

Provided that any equities in respect of the patent may be enforced in like manner as in respect of any other movable property.

Sec.71. Rectification of register by Appellate Board

Sec.72. Register to be open for inspection.

CHAPTER XIV PATENT OFFICE AND ITS ESTABLISHMENT

Sec.73. Controller and other officers.—

(1) The Controller General of Patents, Designs and Trade Marks appointed under sub-section (1) of section 3 of the Trade Marks Act, 1999 (47 of 1999), shall be the Controller of Patents for the purposes of this Act.

(2) For the purposes of this Act, the Central Government may appoint as many examiners and other officers and with such designations as it thinks fit.

(3) Subject to the provisions of this Act, the officers appointed under subsection (2) shall discharge under the superintendence and directions of the Controller such functions of the Controller under this Act as he may, from time to time by general or special order in writing, authorize them to discharge.

Sec.74. Patent office and its branches.—

(1) For the purposes of this Act, there shall be an office which shall be known as the patent office.

(2) The Central Government may, by notification in the Official Gazette, specify the name of the Patent Office.

(3) The head office of the patent office shall be at such place as the Central Government may specify, and for the purpose of facilitating the registration of patents there may be established, at such other places as the Central Government may think fit, branch offices of the patent office.

(4) There shall be a seal of the patent office.

Sec.75. Restriction on employees of patent office as to right or interest in patents.—All officers and employees of the patent office shall be incapable, during the period for which they hold their appointments, to acquire or take, directly or indirectly, except by inheritance or bequest, any right or interest in any patent issued by that office.

Sec.76. Officers and employees not to furnish information, etc.—An officer or employee in the patent office shall not, except when required or authorised by this Act or under a direction in writing of the Central Government or Appellate Board or the Controller or by order of a court,—

(a) furnish information on a matter which is being, or has been, dealt with under this Act ; or

(b) prepare or assist in the preparation of a document required or permitted by or under this Act , to be lodged in the patent office; or

(c) conduct a search in the records of the patent office.

CHAPTER XV POWERS OF CONTROLLER GENERALLY

Sec.77. Controller to have certain powers of **a** civil court.—

(1) Subject to any rules made in this behalf, the Controller in any proceedings before him under this Act shall have the powers of a civil court while trying a suit under the Code of Civil Procedure, 1908 (5 of 1908), in respect of the following matters, namely:—

(*a*) summoning and enforcing the attendance of any person and examining him on oath;

(*b*) requiring the discovery and production of any document;

(*c*) receiving evidence on affidavits;

(*d*) issuing commissions for the examination of witnesses or documents;

(*e*) awarding costs;

(*f*) reviewing his own decision on application made within the prescribed time and in the prescribed manner;

(*g*) setting aside an order passed *ex- parte* on application made within the prescribed time and in the prescribed manner;

(*h*) any other matter which may be prescribed.

(2) Any order for costs awarded by the Controller in exercise of the powers conferred upon him under sub-section (1) shall be executable as a decree of a civil court.

Sec.78. Power of Controller to correct clerical errors etc.—

(1) Without prejudice to the provisions contained in sections 57 and 59 as regards amendment of applications for patents or complete specifications or other documents related thereto and subject to the provisions of section 44, the Controller may, in accordance with the provisions of this section, correct any clerical error in any patent or in any specification or other document filed in pursuance of such application or in any application for a patent or any clerical error in any matter which is entered in the register.

(2) A correction may be made in pursuance of this section either upon a request in writing made by any person interested and accompanied by the prescribed fee, or without such a request.

(3) Where the Controller proposes to make any such correction as aforesaid otherwise than in pursuance of a request made under this section, he shall give notice of the proposal to the patentee or the applicant for the patent, as the case may be, and to any other person who appears to him to be concerned, and shall give them an opportunity to be heard before making the correction.

Sec.79. Evidence how to be given and powers of Controller in respect thereof

Sec.80. Exercise of discretionary powers by Controller

Sec.81. Disposal by Controller of applications for extension of time

CHAPTER XVI WORKING OF PATENTS, COMPULSORY LICENSES AND REVOCATION

Sec.82. Definition of "patented articles" and "patentee".—In this Chapter, unless the context otherwise requires,—

(a) "patented article" includes any article made by a patented process; and

(b) "patentee" includes an exclusive licensee.

Sec.83. General principles applicable to working of patented inventions.—Without prejudice to the other provisions contained in this Act, in exercising the powers conferred by this Chapter, regard shall be had to the following general considerations, namely;—

(*a*) that patents are granted to encourage inventions and to secure that the inventions are worked in India on a commercial scale and to the fullest extent that is reasonably practicable without undue delay;

(*b*) that they are not granted merely to enable patentees to enjoy a monopoly for the importation of the patented article;

(*c*) that the protection and enforcement of patent rights contribute to the promotion of technological innovation and to the transfer and dissemination of technology, to the mutual advantage of producers and users of technological knowledge and in a manner conducive to social and economic welfare, and to a balance of rights and obligations;

(*d*) that patents granted do not impede protection of public health and nutrition and should act as instrument to promote public interest specially in sectors of vital importance for socio-economic and technological development of India;

(*e*) that patents granted do not in any way prohibit Central Government in taking measures to protect public health;

Sec.84. Compulsory licenses.—

(1) At any time after the expiration of three years from the date of the grant of a patent, any person interested may make an application to the Controller for grant of compulsory license on patent on any of the following grounds, namely:—

    (*a*) that the reasonable requirements of the public with respect to the patented invention have not been satisfied,or

    (*b*) that the patented invention is not available to the public at a reasonably affordable price, or

    (*c*) that the patented invention is not worked in the territory of India.

(2) An application under this section may be made by any person notwithstanding that he is already the holder of a license under the patent and no person shall be estopped from alleging that the reasonable requirements of the public with respect to the patented invention are not satisfied or that the patented invention is not worked in the territory of India or that the patented invention is not available to the public at a reasonably affordable price by reason of any admission made by him, whether in such a license or otherwise or by reason of his having accepted such a license.

(3) Every application under sub-section (1) shall contain a statement setting out the nature of the applicant's interest together with such particulars as may be prescribed and the facts upon which the application is based.

Sec.85. Revocation of patents by the Controller for non-working

Sec.86. Power of Controller to adjourn applications for compulsory licenses, etc., in certain cases

Sec.87. Procedure for dealing with applications under sections 84 and 85—

(1) Where the Controller is satisfied, upon consideration of an application under section 84, Or section 85, that a *prima facie* case has been made out for the making of an order, he shall direct the applicant to serve copies of the application upon the patentee and any other person appearing from the register to be interested in the patent in respect of which the application is made, and shall publish the application in the official journal.

(2) The patentee or any other person desiring to oppose the application may, within such time as may be prescribed or within such further time as the Controller may on application (made either before or after the expiration of the prescribed time) allow, give to the Controller notice of opposition.

(3) Any such notice of opposition shall contain a statement setting out the grounds on which the application is opposed.

(4) Where any such notice of opposition is duly given, the Controller shall notify the applicant, and shall give to the applicant and the opponent an opportunity to be heard before deciding the case,

Sec.88. Powers of Controller in granting compulsory licenses.—

(1) Where the Controller is satisfied on an application made under section 84 that the manufacture, use or sale of materials not protected by the patent is prejudiced by reason of conditions imposed by the patentee upon the grant of licenses under the patent, or upon the purchase, hire or use of the patented article or process, he may, subject to the provisions of that section, order the grant of licenses under the patent to such customers of the applicant as he thinks fit as well as to the applicant.

(2) Where an application under section 84 is made by a person being the holder of a license under the patent, the Controller may, if he makes an order for the grant of a license to the applicant, order the existing license to be cancelled, or may, if he thinks fit, instead of making an order for the grant of a license to the applicant, order the existing license to be amended.

(3) Where two or more patents are held by the same patentee and an applicant for a compulsory license establishes that the reasonable requirements of the public have not been satisfied with respect to some only of the said patents, then, if the Controller is satisfied that the applicant cannot efficiently or satisfactorily work the license granted to him under those patents without infringing the other patents held by the patentee and if those patents involve important technical advancement of considerable economic significance in relation to the other patents, he may, by order, direct the grant of a license in respect of the other patents also to enable the licensee to work the patent or patents in regard to which a license is granted under section 84.

(4) Where the terms and conditions of a license have been settled by the Controller, the licensee may, at any time after he has worked the invention on a commercial scale for a period of not less than twelve months, make an application to the Controller for the revision of the terms and conditions on the ground that the terms and conditions settled have proved to be more onerous than originally expected and that in consequence thereof the licensee is unable to work the invention except at a loss:

Provided that no such application shall be entertained a second time.

Sec.89. General purposes for granting compulsory licenses.—The powers of the Controller upon an application made under section 84 shall be exercised with a view to securing the following general purposes, that is to say,—

(*a*) that patented inventions are worked on a commercial scale in the territory of India without undue delay and to the fullest extent that is reasonably practicable;

(*b*) that the interests of any person for the time being working or developing an invention in the territory of India under the protection of a patent are not unfairly prejudiced.

Sec.90. Terms and conditions of compulsory licenses.—(1) In settling the terms and conditions of a license under section 84, the Controller shall Endeavour to secure—

(*i*) that the royalty and other remuneration, if any, reserved to the patentee or other person beneficially entitled to the patent, is reasonable, having regard to the nature of the invention, the expenditure incurred by the patentee in making the invention or in developing it and obtaining a patent and keeping it in force and other relevant factors;

(*ii*) that the patented invention is worked to the fullest extent by the person to whom the license is granted and with reasonable profit to him;

(*iii*) that the patented articles are made available to the public at reasonably affordable prices;

(*iv*) that the license granted is a non-exclusive license;

(*v*) that the right of the licensee is non-assignable;

(*vi*) that the license is for the balance term of the patent unless a shorter term is consistent with public interest;

(*vii*) that the license is granted with a predominant purpose of supply in the Indian market and that the licensee may also export the patented product if need be in accordance with the provisions of sub-clause (iii) of clause (a) of sub-section (7) of section 84;

(*viii*) that in the case of semi-conductor technology, the license granted is to work the invention for public non-commercial use;

(*ix*) that in case the license is granted to remedy a practice etermined after judicial or administrative process to be anti-competitive, the licensee shall be permitted to export the patented product, if need be.

(2) No license granted by the Controller shall authorise the licensee to import the patented article or an article or substance made by a patented process from abroad where such importation would, but for such authorisation, constitute an infringement of the rights of the patentee.

(3) Notwithstanding anything contained in sub-section (2), the Central Government may, if in its opinion it is necessary so to do, in the public interest,direct the Controller at any time to authorise any licensee in respect of a patent to import the patented article or an article or substance made by a patented process from abroad (subject to such conditions as it considers necessary to impose relating among other matters to the royalty and other remuneration, if any, payable to the patentee, the quantum of import, the sale price of the imported article and the period of importation), and thereupon the Controller shall give effect to the directions.

Sec.91. Licensing of related patents

Sec92. Special provision for compulsory licenses on notifications by Central Government

Sec.92A. Compulsory license for export of patented pharmaceutical products in certain exceptional circumstances.

Sec.93. Order for license to operate as a deed between parties concerned.

Sec.94. Termination of compulsory license.—

(1) On an application made by the patentee or any other person deriving title or interest in the patent, a compulsory license granted under section 84 may be terminated by the controller, if and when the circumstances that gave rise to the grant thereof no longer exist and such circumstances are unlikely to recur:

Provided that the holder of the compulsory license shall have the right to object to such termination.

(2) While considering an application under section (1), the Controller shall take into account that the interest of the person who had previously been granted the license is not unduly prejudiced.**95-98.** [Omitted by the *Patents (Amendment) Act,* 2002]

CHAPTER XVII USE OF INVENTIONS FOR PURPOSES OF GOVERNMENT AND ACQUISITION OF INVENTIONS BY CENTRAL GOVERNMENT

Sec.99. Meaning of use of invention for purposes of Government

Sec.100. Power of Central Government to use inventions for purposes of Government

Sec.101. Rights of third parties in respect of use of invention for purposes of Government

Sec.102. Acquisition of inventions and patents by the Central Government

Sec.103. Reference to High Court of disputes as to use for purposes of Government

CHAPTER XVIII SUITS CONCERNING INFRINGEMENT OF PATENTS

Sec104. Jurisdiction.

Sec.104A. Burden of proof in case of suits concerning infringement infringement.—

(1) In any suit for infringement of a patent, where the subject matter of patent is a process for obtaining a product, the court may direct the defendant to prove that the process used by him to obtain the product, identical to the product of the patented process, is different from the patented process if,—

(*a*) the subject matter of the patent is a process for obtaining a new product; or

(*b*) there is a substantial likelihood that the identical product is made by the process, and the patentee or a person deriving title or interest in the patent from him, has been unable through reasonable efforts to determine the process actually used:

Provided that the patentee or a person deriving title or interest in the patent from him first proves that the product is identical to the product directly obtained by the patented process.

(2) In considering whether a party has discharged the burden imposed upon him by sub-section (1), the court shall not require him to disclose any manufacturing or commercial secrets, if it appears to the court that it would be unreasonable to do so.

Sec.105. Power of court to make declaration as to non-infringement

Sec.106. Power of court to grant relief in cases of groundless threats of infringement proceedings.—

(1) Where any person (whether entitled to or interested in a patent or an application for patent or not) threatens any other person by circulars or advertisements or by communications, oral or in writing addressed to that or any other person, with proceedings for infringement of a patent, any person aggrieved thereby may bring a suit against him praying for the following reliefs, that is to say—

(*a*) a declaration to the effect that the threats are unjustifiable;

(*b*) an injunction against the continuance of the threats; and

(*c*) such damages, if any, as he has sustained thereby.

Sec.107. Defences, etc., in suits for infringement.

Sec.107A. Certain acts not to be considered as infringement

Sec.108. Reliefs in suit for infringement.—

(1) The reliefs which a court may grant in any suit for infringement include an injunction (subject to such terms, if any, as the court thinks fit) and, at the option of the plaintiff, either damages or an account of profits.

(2) The court may also order that the goods which are found to be infringing and materials and implements, the predominant use of which is in the creation of infringing goods shall be seized, forfeited or destroyed, as the court deems fit under the circumstances of the case without payment of any compensation.

Sec.109. Right of exclusive licensee to take proceedings against infringement

Sec.110. Right of licensee under section 84 to take proceedings against infringement

Sec.111. Restriction on power of court to grant damages or account of profits for infringement.

Sec.112. Restriction on power of court to grant injunction in certain cases.

Se.c113. Certificate of validity of specification and costs of subsequent suits for infringement thereof.

Sec.114. Relief for infringement of partially valid specification

Sec.115. Scientific advisers.—

(1) In any suit for infringement or in any proceeding before a court under this Act, the court may at any time, and whether or not an application has been made by any party for that purpose, appoint an independent scientific adviser, to assist the court or to inquire and report upon any such question of fact or of opinion (not involving a question of interpretation of law) as it may formulate for the purpose.

(2) The remuneration of the scientific adviser shall be fixed by the court and shall include the costs of making a report and a proper daily fee for any day on which the scientific adviser may be required to attend before the court, and such remuneration shall be defrayed out of moneys provided by Parliament by law for the purpose.

CHAPTER XIX APPEALS TO THE APPELLATE BOARD

Sec.116. Appellate Board.—

(1) Subject to the provisions of this Act, the Appellate Board established under section 83 of the Trade Marks Act, 1999 shall be the Appellate Board for the purposes of this Act and the said Appellate Board shall exercise the jurisdiction, power and authority conferred on it by or under this Act:

Provided that the Technical Member of the Appellate Board for the purposes of this Act shall have the qualifications specified in sub-section.

(2) A person shall not be qualified for appointment as a Technical Member for the purposes of this Act unless he—

(*a*)   has, at least five years held the post of Controller under this Act or has exercised the functions of the Controller under this Act for at least five years; or

(*b*)   has, for at least ten years functioned as a Registered Patent Agent and possesses a degree in engineering or technology or a masters degree in science from any University established under law for the time being in force or equivalent; or

(*c*)   [Omitted by the *Patents (Amendment) Act, 2005*]

Sec.117. Staff of Appellate Board.—

(1)   The Central Government shall determine the nature and categories of the officers and other employees required to assist the Appellate Board in the discharge of its functions under this Act and provide the Appellate Board with such officers and other employees as it may think fit.

(2)   The salaries and allowances and conditions of service of the officers and other employees of the Appellate Board shall be such as may be prescribed.

(3)   The officers and other employees of the Appellate Board shall discharge their functions under the general superintendence of the Chairman of the Appellate Board in the manner as may be prescribed.

Sec.117A. Appeals to Appellate Board

Sec.117B. Procedure and powers of Appellate Board

Sec.117C. Bar of jurisdiction of courts,

Sec.117D. Procedure for application for rectification, etc., before Appellate Board.—

(1)   An application for revocation of a patent before the Appellate Board under section 64 and an application for rectification of the register made to the Appellate Board under section 71 shall be in such form as may be prescribed.

(2)   A certified copy of every order or judgment of the Appellate Board relating to a patent under this Act shall be communicated to the Controller by the Board and the Controller shall give effect to the order of the Board and shall, when so directed, amend the entries in, or rectify, the register in accordance with such order.

Sec.117E. Appearance of Controller in legal proceedings

Sec.117F. Costs of Controller in proceedings before Appellate Board

Sec.117G. Transfer of pending proceedings to Appellate Board

Sec.117H. Power of Appellate Board to make rules.

CHAPTER XX PENALTIES

Sec.118. Contravention of secrecy provisions relating to certain inventions

Sec.119. Falsification of entries in register, etc.—

Sec.120. Unauthorized claim of patent rights.—If any person falsely represents that any article sold by him is patented in India or is the subject of an application for a patent in India, he shall be punishable with fine which may extend to one lakh rupees.

Explanation 1— For the purposes of this section, a person shall be deemed to represent:

(*a*) that an article is patented in India if there is stamped, engraved or impressed on, or otherwise applied to, the article the word "patent" or "patented" or some other word expressing or implying that a patent for the article has been obtained in India;

(*b*) that an article is the subject of an application for a patent in India, if there are stamped, engraved or impressed on, or otherwise applied to, the article the words "patent applied for", "patent pending", or some other words implying that an application for a patent for the article has been made in India.

Sec.121. Wrongful use of words "patent office".—If any person uses on his place of business or any document issued by him or otherwise the words "patent office" or any other words which would reasonably lead to the belief that his place of business is, or is officially connected with, the patent office, he shall be punishable with imprisonment for a term which may extend to six months, or with fine, or with both.

Sec.122. Refusal or failure to supply information

Sec.123. Practice by non-registered patent agents

Sec.124. Offences by companies.—(1) If the person committing an offence under this Act is a company, the company as well as every person in charge of, and responsible to, the company for the conduct of its business at the time of the commission of the offence shall be deemed to be guilty of the offence and shall be liable to be proceeded against and punished accordingly:

Provided that nothing contained in this sub-section shall render any such person liable to any punishment if he proves that the offence was committed without his knowledge or that he exercised all due diligence to prevent the commission of such offence.

CHAPTER XXI PATENT AGENTS

Sec.125. Register of patent agents—

(1) The Controller shall maintain a register to be called the register of patent agents in which shall be entered the names, addresses and other relevant particulars, as may be prescribed, of all persons qualified to have their names so entered under section 126.

(2) Notwithstanding anything contained in sub-section (1), it shall be lawful for the Controller to keep the register of patent agents in computer floppies, diskettes or any other electronic form subject to such safeguards as may be prescribed.

Sec.126. Qualifications for registration as patent agents.—(1) A person shall be qualified to have his name entered in the register of patent agents if he fulfills the following conditions, namely:—

(a) he is a citizen of India;

(b) he has completed the age of 21 years;

(c) he has obtained a degree in science, engineering or technology from any university established under law for the time being in force in the territory of India or possesses such other equivalent qualifications as the Central Government may specify in this behalf,

CHAPTER XXII INTERNATIONAL ARRANGEMENTS

IT Act 2000

Sec. 1. Short title, extent, commencement and application.—

(1) This Act may be called the Information Technology Act, 2000.

(2) It shall extend to the whole of India and, save as otherwise provided in this Act, it applies also to any offence or contravention there under committed outside India by any person.

(3) It shall come into force on such date1 as the Central Government may, by notification, appoint and different dates may be appointed for different provisions of this Act and any reference in any such provision to the commencement of this Act shall be construed as a reference to the commencement of that provision.

Definitions.—

(1) In this Act, unless the context otherwise requires:

(a) *"access* " with its grammatical variations and cognate expressions means gaining entry into, instructing or communicating with the logical, arithmetical, or memory function resources of a computer, computer system or computer network;

(b) *"addressee"* means a person who is intended by the originator to receive the electronic record but does not include any intermediary;

(*c*) "***adjudicating officer*** " means an adjudicating officer appointed under subsection (*1*) *of* section 46;

(*d*) "***affixing*** 3[***electronic signature***]" with its grammatical variations and cognate expressions means adoption of any methodology or procedure by a person for the purpose of authenticating an electronic record by means of 4[*electronic signature*];

(*e*) "***appropriate Government*** " means as respects any matter,—

  (*i*) enumerated in List II of the Seventh Schedule to the Constitution;

  (*ii*) relating to any State law enacted under List III of the Seventh Schedule to the Constitution, the State Government and in any other case, the Central Government;

(*f*) "***asymmetric crypto system*** " means a system of a secure key pair consisting of a private key for creating a digital signature and a public key to verify the digital signature;

(*g*) "***Certifying Authority*** " means a person who has been granted a license to issue a [electronic signature] Certificate under section 24;

(*h*) "***certification practice statement*** " means a statement issued by a Certifying Authority to specify the practices that the Certifying Authority employs in issuing 6[Electronic Signature]Certificates; 7[(*ha*) "***communication device*** " means cell phones, personal digital assistance or combination of both or any other device used to communicate, send or transmit any text, video, audio or image;]

(*i*) "***computer*** " means any electronic, magnetic, optical or other high-speed data processing device or system which performs logical, arithmetic, and memory functions by manipulations of electronic, magnetic or optical impulses, and includes all input, output, processing, storage, computer software, or communication facilities which are connected or related to the computer in a computer system or computer network;

(*j*) "***computer network*** " means the inter-connection of one or more computers or computer systems or communication device through—

  (*i*) the use of satellite, microwave, terrestrial line, wire, wireless orother communication media;

  (*ii*) terminals or a complex consisting of two or more inter-connected computers or communication device whether or not the interconnection is continuously maintained;]

(*k*) "***computer resource*** " means computer, computer system, computer network,data, computer data-base or software;

(*l*) "***computer system*** " means a device or collection of devices, including input and output support devices and excluding calculators which are not programmable and capable of being used in conjunction with external files, which contain computer programmes, electronic instructions, input data, and output data, that performs logic, arithmetic, data storage and retrieval, communication control and other functions;

(*m*) "***Controller*** " means the Controller of Certifying Authorities appointed under sub-section (*7*) of section 17;

(*n*) *"Cyber Appellate Tribunal* " means the Cyber 9[. . . .] Appellate Tribunal established under sub-section (*1*) of section 48;

10[(*na*) *"cyber cafe* " means any facility from where access to the internet is offered by any person in the ordinary course of business to the members of the public;

(*nb*) *"cyber security* " means protecting information, equipment, devices, computer, computer resource, communication device and information stored therein from unauthorised access, use, disclosure, disruption, modification or destruction;]

(*o*) *"data* " means a representation of information, knowledge, facts, concepts or instructions which are being prepared or have been prepared in a formalised manner, and is intended to be processed, is being processed or has been processed in a computer system or computer network, and may be in any form (including computer printouts, magnetic or optical storage media, punched cards, punched tapes) or stored internally in the memory of the computer;

(*p*) *"digital signature* " means authentication of any electronic record by a subscriber by means of an electronic method or procedure in accordance with the provisions of section 3;

(*q*) *"Digital Signature Certificate* " means a Digital Signature Certificate issued under sub-section (*4*) *of* section 35;

(*r*) *"electronic form* " with reference to information means any information generated, sent, received or stored in media, magnetic, optical, computer memory, micro film, computer generated micro fiche or similar device;

(*s*) *"Electronic Gazette* " means the official gazette published in the electronic form;

(*t*) *"electronic record* " means data, record or data generated, image or sound stored, received or sent in an electronic form or micro film or computer generated micro fiche;

11 [(*ta*) *"electronic signature* " means authentication of any electronic record by a subscriber by means of the electronic technique specified in the Second

Schedule and includes digital signature;

(*ta*) *"Electronic Signature Certificate* " means an Electronic Signature Certificate issued under Section 35 and includes Digital Signature Certificate;]

(*u*) *"function* ", in relation to a computer, includes logic, control, arithmetical process, deletion, storage and retrieval and communication or telecommunication from or within a computer

12[(*ua*) *"Indian Computer Emergency Response Team* " means an agency established under sub-section (1) of section 70B;] (*v*) *"information* " includes 13[data, message, text,] images, sound, voice, codes, computer programmes, software and data-bases or micro film or computer generated micro fiche ;

14[(*w*) *"intermediary* ", with respect to any particular electronic records, means any person who on behalf of another person receives, stores or transmits that record or provides any service with respect to that record and includes telecom service providers, network service providers, internet service providers, web-hosting service providers, search engines, online payment sites, onlineauction sites, online-market places and cyber cafes;]

(*v*) **"key pair** ", in an asymmetric crypto system, means a private key and its mathematically related public key, which are so related that the public key can verify a digital signature created by the private key;

(*w*) **"law** " includes any Act of Parliament or of a State Legislature, Ordinances promulgated by the President or a Governor, as the case may be, Regulations made by the President under article 240, Acts enacted as President's Act under sub-clause (*a*) of clause (*1*) of article 357 of the Constitution and includes rules, regulations, bye-laws and orders issued or made thereunder;

(*x*) **"license** " means a license granted to a Certifying Authority under section 24;

(*xa*) **"originator** " means a person who sends, generates, stores or transmits any electronic message or causes any electronic message to be sent, generated, stored or transmitted to any other person but does not include an intermediary;

(*xb*) **"prescribed** " means prescribed by rules made under this Act;

(*xc*) **"private key** " means the key of a key pair used to create a digital signature;

(*xd*) **"public key** " means the key of a key pair used to verify a digital signature and listed in the Digital Signature Certificate;

(*xe*) **"secure system** " means computer hardware, software, and procedure that—

    (*a*)   are reasonably secure from unauthorised access and misuse;

    (*b*)   rovide a reasonable level of reliability and correct operation;

    (*c*)   are reasonably suited to performing the intended functions; and

    (*d*)   adhere to generally accepted security procedures;

(*xf*) **"security procedure** " means the security procedure prescribed under section 16 by the Central Government;

(*xg*) **"subscriber** " means a person in whose name the 15[Electronic Signature] Certificate is issued;

(*xh*) **"verify** " in relation to a digital signature, electronic record or public key, with its grammatical variations and cognate expressions means to determine whether—

    (*a*)   the initial electronic record was affixed with the digital signature by the use of private key corresponding to the public key of the subscriber;

    (*b*)   the initial electronic record is retained intact or has been altered since such electronic record was so affixed with the digital signature.

(2) Any reference in this Act to any enactment or any provision thereof shall, in relation to an area in which such enactment or such provision is not in force, be construed as a reference to the corresponding law or the relevant provision of the corresponding law, if any, in force in that area.

Chapter 2. **DIGITAL SIGNATURE AND ELECTRONIC SIGNATURE**

This chapter describes the provisons regarding the Authentication of electronic records and digital signature

Sec. 3. Authentication of electronic records—

(1) Subject to the provisions of this section any subscriber may authenticate an electronic record by affixing his digital signature.

(2) The authentication of the electronic record shall be effected by the use of asymmetric crypto system and hash function which envelop and transform the initial electronic record into another electronic record.

Explanation.—For the purposes of this sub-section, "hash function" means an algorithm mapping or translation of one sequence of bits into another, generally smaller, set known as "hash result" such that an electronic record yields the same hash result every time the algorithm is executed with the same electronic record as its input making it computationally infeasible —

(*a*) To derive or reconstruct the original electronic record from the hash result produced by the algorithm;

(*b*) that two electronic records can produce the same hash result using the algorithm.

(3) Any person by the use of a public key of the subscriber can verify the electronic record.

(4) The private key and the public key are unique to the subscriber and constitute a functioning key pair.

CHAPTER 3 ELECTRONIC GOVERNANCE

Chapter III of the Act is one of the most important chapters in the Act. This Chapter specifies the procedure to be followed for sending and receiving of electronic record and the time and place of the despatch and receipt. This Chapter contains sections 4 to 10.

Sec. 4. Legal recognition of electronic records

Sec. 5. Legal recognition of 18[electronic signatures

Sec. 6. Use of electronic records and 20[electronic signatures] in Government and its agencies

Sec. 6 A. Delivery of service by service provider.

Sec. 7.Retention of electronic records.

Sec. 7 A. Audit of documents etc., maintained in electronic form.

Sec. 8. Publication of rule, regulation, etc., in Electronic Gazette.

Sec. 9. Sections 6, 7 and 8 not to confer right to insist document should be accepted in electronic form.

Sec. 10. Power to make rules by Central Government in respect of 23[electronic

Signature.

Sec. 10. A. Validity of contracts formed through electronic means.

CHAPTER 4 ATTRIBUTION, ACKNOWLEDGMENT AND DISPATCH OF ELECTRONIC RECORDS

This chapter explain the provison related to the electronic records and authentication.

Sec. 11. Attribution of electronic records.

Sec. 12. Acknowledgment of Receipt.

S. 13. Time and place of dispatch and receipt of electronic record.

CHAPTER 5 SECURE ELECTRONIC RECORDS AND SECUE ELECTRONIC SIGNATURES

This chapter contains the provison of secure electronic records.

Sec. 14. Secure electronic record.

Sec. 15. Secure electronic signature.

Sec. 16. Security procedure and practices.

CHAPTER 6 REGULATION OF CERTIFYING AUTHORITIES

This chapter contains the provisions regarding the appointment, functions of controllers and Recognition of foreign Certifying Authorities.

Sec. 17. Appointment of Controller and other officers

Sec. 18. Functions of Controller

Sec. 19. Recognition of foreign Certifying Authorities

Sec. 20. Controller to act as repository

Sec. 21. License to issue 34[Electronic Signature] Certificates

Sec. 22. Application for License

Sec. 23. Renewal of License

Sec. 24. Procedure for grant or rejection of License.

Sec. 25. Suspension of LicenseS. 26. Notice of suspension or revocation of license

Sec. 27. Power to delegate

Sec. 28. Power to investigate contraventions.

Sec. 29. Access to computers and data

Sec. 30. Certifying Authority to follow certain procedures

Sec. 31. Certifying Authority to ensure compliance of the Act,

Sec. 32. Display of license

Sec. 33. Surrender of license

Sec. 34. Disclosure

CHAPTER 7 [ELECTRONIC SIGNATURE] CERTIFICATES

This chapter contains the provisions regarding issuing certificate and suspension. Revocation of digital signature certificate.

Sec. 35. Certifying Authority to issue 46[Electronic Signature] Certificate

Sec. 36. Representations upon issuance of Digital Signature Certificate

Sec. 37. Suspension of Digital Signature Certificate.

Sec. 38. Revocation of Digital Signature Certificate

CHAPTER 8 DUTIES OF SUBSCRIBERS

This chapter contains the provisions regarding Duties of subscriber of Electronic Signature Certificate and Acceptance of Digital Signature Certificate

Sec. 40. Generating key pair

Sec. 40A. Duties of subscriber of Electronic Signature Certificate

Sec. 41. Acceptance of Digital Signature Certificate

Sec 42. Control of private key

CHAPTER 9 [PENALTIES, COMPENSATION AND ADJUDICATION]

This chapter contains the provisions regarding Penalty and compensation for damage and Compensation for failure to protect data.

Sec. 43. 57[Penalty and compensation] for damage to computer, computer system,etc

Sec. 43A. Compensation for failure to protect data

Sec. 44. Penalty for failure to furnish information, return, etc.

Sec. 45. Residuary penalty

Sec. 46. Power to adjudicate

Sec. 47. Factors to be taken into account by the adjudicating officer

CHAPTER 10 THE CYBER APPELLATE TRIBUNAL

This chapter contains the provisions regarding Establishment , Composition of Cyber Appellate Tribunal and powers of Tribunal

Sec. 48. Establishment of Cyber Appellate Tribunal.

Sec. 49. Composition of Cyber Appellate Tribunal.

Sec. 50. Qualifications for appointment as Chairperson and Members of Cyber Appellate Tribunal

Sec. 51. Term of office, conditions of service, etc., of Chairperson and Members.

CHAPTER 11 OFFENCES

This chapter contains the provisions regarding computer related offences and punishments.

Sec. 65. Tampering with computer source documents.—Whoever knowingly or intentionally conceals, destroys or alters or intentionally or knowingly causes another to conceal, destroy or alter any computer source code used for a computer, computer programme, computer system or computer network, when the computer source code is required to be kept or maintained by law for the time being in force, shall be punishable with imprisonment up to three years, or with fine which may extend up to two lakh rupees, or with both.

Explanation.—For the purposes of this section, "computer source code" means the listing of programmes, computer Commands, design and layout and programme analysis of computer resource in any form. 66

Sec. 66. Computer related offences.—If any person, dishonestly or fraudulently, does any act referred to in section 43, he shall be punishable with imprisonment for a term which may extend to three years or with fine which may extend to five lakh rupees or with both.

Explanation.—For the purpose of this section,—

(*a*) the word "dishonesty" shall have the meaning assigned to it in section 24 of the Indian Penal Code (45 of 1860).

(*b*) the word "fraudulently" shall have the meaning assigned to it in section 25 of the Indian Penal Code (45 of 1860).

Sec. 66A. Punishment for sending offensive messages through communication

service, etc.—Any person who sends, by means of a computer resource or a communication device,—

(*a*) any information that is grossly offensive or has meaning character, or

(*b*) any information which he knows to be false, but for the purpose of causing annoyance, inconvenience, danger, obstruction, insult, injury, criminal intim- idation, enmity, hatred or ill will, persistently by making use of such computer resource or a communication device; or

(*c*) any electronic mail or electronic mail massage for the purpose of causing annoyance or inconvenience or to deceive or to mislead the addressee or recipient about the origin of such massage, shall be punishable with imprisonment for a term which may extend to three years and with fine.

Explanation.—For the purposes of this section, terms "electronic mail" and "electronic mail message" means a message or information created to transmitted or received on a computer, computer system, computer resource or communication device including attachments in text, image, audio, video and any other electronic record, which may be transmitted with the message.

Sec. 66B. Punishment for dishonestly receiving stolen computer resource or

communication device.—Whoever dishonestly receives or retains any stolen computer

resource or communication device knowing or having reason to believe the same to be stolen computer resource or communication device, shall be punished with imprisonment of either description for a term which may extend to three years or with fine which may extend to rupees one lakh or with both.

Sec. 66C. Punishment for identity theft.—Whoever, fraudulently or dishonestly make use of the electronic signature, password or any other unique identification feature of any other person, shall be punished with imprisonment of either description for a term which may extend to three years and shall also be liable to fine which may extend to rupees one lakh.

Sec. 66D. Punishment for cheating by personation by using computer resource.—

Whoever, by means of any communication device or computer resource cheats by personation, shall be punished with imprisonment of either description for a term which may extend to three years and shall also be liable to fine which may extend to one lakh rupees.

Sec. 66E. Punishment for violation of privacy.—Whosoever, intentionally or knowingly captures, publishes or transmits the image of a private area of any person without his or her consent, under circumstances violating the privacy of that person, shall be punished with imprisonment which may extend to three years or with fine not exceeding two lakh rupees, or with both.

Explanation.—Fro the purposes of this section—

(*a*) "transmit" means to electronically send a visual image with the internet that it be viewed by a person or persons;

(*b*) "capture", with respect to an image, means to videotape, photograph, film or record by any means;

(*c*) "private area" means the naked or undergarment clad genitals, public area, buttocks or female breast;

(*d*) "publishes" means reproduction in the printed or electronic form and making it available for public;

(*e*) "under circumstances violating privacy" means circumstances in which a person can have a reasonable expectation that—

(*i*) he or she could disrobe in privacy, without being concerned that an image of his private area was being captured; or

(*ii*) any part of his or her private area would not be visible to the public regardless of whether that person is in a public or private place.

Sec. 66F. Punishment for cyber terrorism.—(1) Whosoever,—

(*A*) with intent to threaten the unity, integrity, security or sovereignty of India or to strike terror in the people or any section of the people by—

(*i*) denying or cause the denial of access to any person authorised to access computer resource; or

(*ii*) attempting to penetrate or access a computer resource without authorisation or exceeding authorised access; or

(*iii*) introducing or causing to introduce any computer contaminant, and by means of such conduct causes or is likely to cause death or injuries to persons or damage to or destruction of property or disputes or knowing that it is likely to cause damage or disruption of supplies or services essential to the life of the community or adversely affect the critical information infrastructure specified under section 70; or

(*B*) knowingly or intentionally penetrates or accesses a computer resource without authorisation or exceeding authorised access, and by means of such conduct obtains access to information, data or computer database that is restricted for reasons of the security of the state or foreign relations; or any restricted information, data or computer database, with reasons to believe that such information, data or computer database so obtained may be used to cause or likely to cause injury to the interests of the sovereignty and integrity of India, the security of the State, friendly relations with foreign States, public order, decency or morality, or in relation to contempt of court, defamation or incitement to an offence, or to the advantage of any foreign nation, group of individuals or otherwise, commits the offence of cyber terrorism.

(2) whoever commits or conspires to commit cyber terrorism shall be punishable with imprisonment which may extend to imprisonment for life. 67

Sec. 67. Punishment for publishing or transmitting obscene material in electronic form.—

Whoever publishes or transmits or causes to be published or transmitted in the electronic form, any material which is lascivious or appeals to the prurient interest or if its effect is such as to tend to deprave and corrupt persons who are likely, having regard to all relevant circumstances, to read, see or hear the matter contained or embodied in it, shall be punished on first conviction with imprisonment of either description for a term which may extend to three years and with fine which may extend to five lakh rupees and in the event of a second or subsequent conviction with imprisonment of either description for a term which may extend to five years and also with fine which may extend to ten lakh rupees.

Sec. 67A. Punishment for publishing or transmitting of material containing sexually

explicit act, etc., in electronic form.—Whoever publishes or transmits or causes to be published or transmitted in the electronic form any material which contains sexually explicit act or conduct shall be punished on first conviction with imprisonment of either description for a term which may extend to five years and with fine which may extend to ten lakh rupees and in the event of second or subsequent conviction with imprisonment of either description for a term which may extend to seven years and also with fine which may extend to ten lakh rupees.

Sec. 67B. Punishment for publishing or transmitting of material depicting children

in sexually explicit act, etc., in electronic form.—Whoever—

(*a*) publishes or transmits or causes to be published or transmitted material in any electronic form which depicts children engaged in sexually explicit act or conduct; or

(*b*) creates text or digital images, collects, seeks, browses, downloads, advertises, promotes, exchanges or distributes material in any electronic form depicting children in obscene or indecent or sexually explicit manner; or

(*c*) cultivates, entices or induces children to online relationship which one or more children for and on sexually explicit act or in a manner that may offend a reasonable adult on the computer resource; or

(*d*) facilitates abusing children online; or

(*e*) records in any electronic form own abuse or that of others pertaining to sexually explicit act with children,shall be punished on first conviction with imprisonment of either description for a term which may extend to five year and with fine which may extend to ten lakh rupees and in the event of second or subsequent conviction with imprisonment of either description for a term which may extend to seven years and also with fine which may extend to ten lakh rupees;

Provided that provisions of section 67, section 67A and this section does not extend to

any book, pamphlet, paper, writing, drawing, painting representation or figure in electronic

form—

(*i*) the publication of which is proved to be justified as being for the public good on the ground that such book, pamphlet, paper, writing, drawing, painting representation or figure is in the interest of science, literature, art or learning or other objects of general concern; or

(*ii*) which is kept or used for *bona fide* heritage or religious purpose.

Explanation—For the purpose of this section, "children" means a person who has not

completed the age of 18 years.

Sec. 67C. Preservation and retention of information by intermediaries.—(1) Intermediary

shall preserve and retain such information as may be specified for such duration and in such manner and format as the Central Government may prescribed. (2) Any intermediary who intentionally or knowingly contravenes the provisions of sub-section (1) shall be punished with an imprisonment for a term which may extend to three years and shall also be liable to fine.]

Sec. 68. Power of the Controller to give directions.—(1) The Controller may, by order,direct a Certifying Authority or any employee of such Authority to take such measures or cease carrying on such activities as specified in the order if those are necessary to ensure compliance with the provisions of this Act, rules or any regulations made there under.

81[(2) Any person who intentionally or knowingly fails to comply with any order under sub-section (1) shall be guilty of an offence and shall be liable on conviction to imprisonment for a term not exceeding two years or a fine not exceeding one lakh rupees or with both.] 69

Sec. 69. Power to issue directions for interception or monitoring or decryption **of any information through any computer resource.**—(1) Where the Central Government or a State Government or any of its officers specially authorised by the Central Government or the State Government, as the case may be, in this behalf may, if satisfied that it is necessary or expedient so to do, in the interest of the sovereignty or integrity of India, defence of India, security of the State, friendly relations with foreign States or public order or for preventing incitement to the commission of any cognizable offence relating to above or for investigation of any offence, it may subject to the provisions of sub-section (2), for reasons to be recorded in writing by order, direct any agency of the appropriate Government to intercept, monitor or decrypt or cause to be intercepted or monitored or decrypted any information generated, transmitted, received or stored in any computer resource.

(2) The procedure and safeguards subject to which such interception or monitoring or decryption may be carried out, shall be such as may be prescribed.

(3) The subscriber or intermediary or any person in-charge of the computer resource shall, when called upon by any agency referred to in sub-section (1) extend all facilities

and technical assistance to—

(*a*) provide access to or secure access to the computer resource generating transmitting, receiving or storing such information; or

(*b*) intercept, monitor, or decrypt the information, as the case may be; or

(*c*) provide information stored in computer resource.

(4) The subscriber or intermediary or any person who fails to assist the agency referred to in sub-section (3) shall be punished with imprisonment for a term which may extend to seven years and shall also be liable to fine.

S. 69 A. Power to issue directions for blocking public access of any information through any computer resource.—(1) Where the Central Government or any of its officers specially authorised by it in this behalf is satisfied that it is necessary or expedient so to do, in the interest of sovereignty and integrity of India, defence of India, security of the State, friendly relations with forei*gn States or public order or for preventing incitement to the commission of any cognizable offence relating to above, it may subject to the provisions of sub-section (2), for reasons to be recorded in writing by order, direct any agency of the Government or intermediary to block for access by the public any information generated, transmitted, received or stored in any computer resource.

(2) The procedure and safeguards subject to which such blocking for access by the public may be carried out, shall be such as may be prescribed.

(3) The intermediary who fails to comply with the direction issued under sub-section

(1) shall be punished with an imprisonment for a term which may extend to seven years and shall also be liable to fine. S. 69B. Power to authorise to monitor and collect traffic data or information

through any computer resource for cyber security.—(1) The Central Government may, to enhance cyber security and for identification analysis and prevention of intrusion or spread of computer containment in the country, by notification in the Official Gazette, authorise any agency of the Government to monitor and collect traffic data or information generated, transmitted, received or stored in any computer resource.

(2) The intermediary or any person in-charge or the computer resource shall, when called upon by the agency which has been authorised under sub-section (1), provide technical assistance and extend all facilities to such agency to enable online access or to secure and provide online access to the computer resource generating, transmitting, receiving or storing such traffic data or information.

(3) The procedure and safeguards for monitoring and collecting traffic data or information,

shall be such as may be prescribed.

(4) Any intermediary who intentionally or knowingly contravenes the provisions of sub-section (2) shall be punished with an imprisonment for a term which any extend to three years and shall also be liable to fine.

Explanation.—For the purpose of this section,—

(*i*) "computer contaminant" shall have the meaning assigned to it in section 43;

(*ii*) "traffic data" means any data identifying or purporting to identify any person, computer system or computer network or location to or from which the communication is or may be transmitted and includes communications origin, destination, route, time, date, size, duration or type of underlying service and any other information.] 70

Sec. 70. Protected system.—83[(1) The appropriate Government may, by notification in the Official Gazette, declare that any computer resource which directly or indirectly affects the facility of Critical Information Infrastructure, to be a protected system.

Explanation.—For the purposes of this section, "Critical Information Infrastructure" means the computer resource, the incapacitation or destruction of which, shall have debilitating impact on national security, economy, public health or safety.]

(2) The appropriate Government may, by order in writing, authorise the persons who are authorised to access protected systems notified under sub-section (*1*).

(3) Any person who secures access or attempts to secure access to a protected system\ in contravention of the provisions of this section shall be punished with imprisonment of either description for a term which may extend to ten years and shall also be liable to fine.

(4) The Central Government shall prescribe the information security practices and procedures for such protected system.]

Sec. 70A. National nodal agency.—(1) The Central Government may, by notification published in the Official Gazette, designate any organisation of the Government as the national nodal agency in respect of Critical Information Infrastructure Protection.

(2) The national nodal agency designated under sub-section (1) shall be responsiblefor all measures including Research and Development relating to protection of Critical Information Infrastructure.

(3) The manner of performing functions and duties of the agency referred to in subsection

(1) shall be such as may be prescribed.

Sec. 70B. Indian Computer Emergency Response Team to serve as national

agency for incident response.—

(1) The Central Government shall, by notification in the Official Gazette, appoint an agency of the Government to be called the Indian Computer Emergency Response Team.

(2) The Central Government shall provide the agency referred to in sub-section (1) with a Director-General and such other officers and employees as may be prescribed .

(3) The salary and allowances and terms and conditions of the Director-General and other officers and employees shall be such as may be prescribed.

(4) The Indian Computer Emergency Response Team shall serve as the national agency for performing the following functions in the area of cyber security.—

　(*a*)　collection, analysis and dissemination of information on cyber incidents;

　(*b*)　forecast and alerts of cyber security incidents;

　(*c*)　emergency measures for handling cyber security incidents;

　(*d*)　coordination of cyber incidents response activities;

　(*e*)　issue guidelines, advisors, vulnerability notes and whitepapers relating to information security practices, procedures, prevention, response and reporting of cyber incidents;

　(*f*)　such other functions relating to cyber security as may be prescribed.

(5) The manner of performing functions and duties of the agency referred to in subsection

　(1)　shall be such as may be prescribed.

(6) For carrying out the provisions of sub-section (4), the agency referred to in subsection

　(1)　may call for information and give direction to the service providers, intermediaries, data centers, body corporate and any other person.

(7) Any service provider intermediaries, data centers, body corporate or person who fails to provide the information called for the comply with the direction under subsection

(6) shall be punishable with imprisonment for a term which may be extend to one year with fine which may extend to one lakh rupees or with both.

(8) No court shall take cognizance of any offence under this section, except on a complaint made by an officer authorised in this behalf by the agency referred to in subsection (1).] 71

Sec. 71. Penalty for misrepresentation.—Whoever makes any misrepresentation to, or suppresses any material fact from, the Controller or the Certifying Authority for obtaining any license or 86[Electronic Signature] Certificate, as the case may be, shall be punished with imprisonment for a term which may extend to two years, or with fine which may extend to one lakh rupees, or with both. 72

Sec. 72. Penalty for breach of confidentiality and privacy.—Save as otherwise provided in this Act or any other law for the time being in force, any person who, in pursuant of any of the powers conferred under this Act, rules or regulations made thereunder, has secured access to any electronic record, book, register, correspondence, information, document or other material without the consent of the person concerned discloses such electronic record, book, register, correspondence, information, document or other material to any other person shall be punished with imprisonment for a term which may extend to two years, or with fine which may extend to one lakh rupees, or with both.

Sec. 72A. Punishment for disclosure of information in breach of lawful contract.—

Save as otherwise provided in this Act or any other law for the time being in force, any person including and intermediary who, while providing services under the terms of lawful contract, has secured access to any material containing personal information about another person, with the intent to cause or knowing that he is likely to cause wrongful loss or wrongful gain discloses, without the consent of the person concerned, or in breach of a lawful contract, such material to any other person, shall be punished with imprisonment for a term which may extend to three years, or with fine which may extend to five lakh rupees, or with both.] 73

Sec. 73. Penalty for publishing 88[Electronic Signature] Certificate false in certain

particulars.—(1) No person shall publish a 89[Electronic Signature] Certificate or otherwise make it available to any other person with the knowledge that—

(*a*) the Certifying Authority listed in the certificate has not issued it; or

(*b*) the subscriber listed in the certificate has not accepted it; or (c) the certificate has been revoked or suspended, unless such publication is for the purpose of verifying a 90[electronic signature] created prior to such suspension or revocation

(2) Any person who contravenes the provisions of sub-section (*1*) shall be punished with imprisonment for a term which may extend to two years, or with fine which may extend to one lakh rupees, or with both. 74

Sec. 74. Publication for fraudulent purpose.—Whoever knowingly creates, publishes or otherwise makes available a 91[Electronic Signature] Certificate for any fraudulent or unlawful purpose shall be punished with imprisonment for a term which may extend to two years, or with fine which may extend to one lakh rupees, or with both. 75

Sec. 75. Act to apply for offences or contravention committed outside India.—(1)

Subject to the provisions of sub-section (*2*), the provisions of this Act shall apply also to

any offence or contravention committed outside India by any person irrespective of his

nationality.

(2) For the purposes of sub-section (*1*), this Act shall apply to an offence or contravention committed outside India by any person if the act or conduct constituting the offence or contravention involves a computer, computer system or computer network located in India. 76

Sec. 76. Confiscation.—Any computer, computer system, floppies, compact disks, tape drives or any other accessories related thereto, in respect of which any provision of this Act, rules, orders or regulations made thereunder has been or is being contravened, shall be liable to confiscation: *Provided* that where it is established to the satisfaction of the court adjudicating the confiscation that the person in whose possession, power or control of any such computer, computer system, floppies, compact disks, tape drives or any other accessories relating thereto is found is not responsible for the contravention of the provisions of this Act, rules, orders or regulations made thereunder, the court may, instead of making an order for confiscation of such computer, computer system, floppies, compact disks, tape drives or any other accessories related thereto, make such other order authorised by this

Act against the person contravening of the provisions of this Act, rules, orders or regulations made thereunder as it may think fit.

Sec. 77. Compensation penalties or confiscation not to interfere with other

punishment.—No compensation awarded, penalty imposed or confiscation made under this Act shall prevent the award of compensation or imposition of any other penalty or punishment under any other law for the time being in force.

Sec. 77A. Compounding of offences.—

(1) A court of competent jurisdiction may compound offences, other than offences for which the punishment for life or imprisonment for a term exceeding three years has been provided, under this Act: *Provided* that the court shall not compound such offences where the accused is, by reason of his previous conviction, liable to either enhance punishment or to a punishment of a different kind:

Provided further that the court shall not compound any offence where such offence affects the socio economic conditions of the country or has been committed against a child below the age of 18 years or a woman.

(2) The person accused of an offence under this Act may file an application for compounding in the court in which offence is pending for trial and the provisions of section 265B and 265C of the Code of Criminal Procedure, 1973 (2 of 1974) shall apply.

Sec. 77B. Offences with three years imprisonment to be bailable.— Notwithstanding

Anything contained in the Code of Criminal Procedure, 1973 (2 of 1974), the offence punishable with imprisonment of three years and above shall be cognizable and the offence punishable with imprisonment of three years shall be bailable.]

Sec. 78. Power to investigate offences.—Notwithstanding anything contained in the Code of Criminal Procedure, 1973 (2 of 1974), a police officer not below the rank of 93[Inspector] shall investigate any offence under this Act.

Chapter 12 INTERMEDIARIES NOT TO BE LIABLE IN CERTAIN CASES

Sec. 79. Exemption from liability of intermediary in certain cases.

CHAPTER 12A EXAMINER OR ELECTRONIC EVIDENCE

Sec. 79A. Central Government to notify Examiner of Electronic Evidence

CHAPTER 13 MISCELLANEOUS

This chapter contains the miscellaneous provisons.

Software Licensing

Software is governed by copyright law. a software program is a "work" recognized and protected by the *Copyright Act* (Canada). As a result, the owner of the copyright has the sole right to control use and reproduction of the software.

Software owners can grant licenses. A license is a transfer of less than all the owner's rights. A license is simply a limited right to use the property of another. In the case of software, it is the right to use the software. A license to use is purely contractual and there are no implied rights of use, so if a license agreement doesn't grant a particular right, then the licensee (user) doesn't have that right.

Who can use software?

Properly describing whose use is permitted, and whose use isn't permitted, is critical to a software license. Is use limited to one computer, or can it can be used on multiple computers in a network? Is the license count based on total "seats" or total "users" (and can the licensee change users)? Is there a limit on multiple concurrent users? Instead of controlling seats or users, is the license available to everyone at one physical site (a site license) or is it available to everyone in the business (an enterprise license)?

Other important license terms

The owner and user should clearly state the license fee, and whether the license is time-limited or perpetual, transferable or restricted, and irrevocable or revocable.

The owner will want limitations on the user's ability to transfer the software (either by assignments or sublicenses). Some licenses state that a merger or change of corporate control in user triggers license termination, or a substantial transfer fee.

Owners often include a covenant by the user to not copy the software (other than perhaps one backup copy). Due to the many variables which can adversely affect the expected performance of software, owners usually will not give any performance representations. Owners typically require that the licenseecovenant to not reverse engineer the software, and will prohibit user modifications.

Maintenance

Users often will require maintenance services, which typically are priced as a percentage of the original license price. Users should seek to ensure that they get value for the fees they pay, which can include basic help services (whether online or by help desk telephone) with specified response times and escalation of response, bug fixes, updates and upgrades, and support and correction for major errors and significant problems.

Software Infringement

Much software is now purchased online, with users blithely clicking the "I Agree" button without reading and considering the terms of purchase. This can be risky, because a breach of license terms can be an offence under the Copyright Act,

Recommendation

Owners should ensure that they have well-drafted, • suitable licenses for use with their customers

Users know the limitations on their scope of use, copying • and transfer of the software

Users should monitor and police their own use, so as • to avoid inadvertently exposing themselves to copyright infringement prosecution.

ISO(International Standard Organization)

Information security plays an important role in protecting the assets of an organisation. As no single formula can guarantee 100% security, there is a need for a set of benchmarks or standards to help ensure an adequate level of security is attained, resources are used efficiently, and the best security practices are adopted.

To address the situation, a number of governments and organisations have set up benchmarks, standards and in some cases, legal regulations on information security to help ensure an adequate level of security is maintained, resources are used in the right way, and the best security practices are adopted.

"The International Organisation for Standardisation (ISO), established in 1947, is a non-governmental international body that collaborates with the International Electrotechnical Commission (IEC)3 and the International Telecommunication Union (ITU)4 on information and communications technology (ICT) standards5".

The following are commonly referenced ISO security standards:

1. ISO/IEC 27002:2005 (Code of Practice for Information Security Management)

This standard contains guidelines and best practices recommendations for these 10 security domains:

(*a*) security policy;

(*b*) organisation of information security;

(*c*) asset management;

(*d*) human resources security;

(*e*) physical and environmental security;

(*f*) communications and operations management;

(*g*) access control;

(*h*) information systems acquisition, development and maintenance;

(*i*) information security incident management;

(*j*) business continuity management; and

(*k*) compliance.

2. ISO/IEC 27001:2005 (Information Security Management System - Requirements)

The standard introduces a cyclic model known as the "Plan-Do-Check-Act" (PDCA) model that aims to establish, implement, monitor and improve the effectiveness of an organisation's ISMS. The PDCA cycle has these four phases:

(*a*) "Plan" phase – establishing the ISMS (Information Security Management System)

(*b*) "Do" phase – implementing and operating the ISMS

(*c*) "Check" phase – monitoring and reviewing the ISMS

(*d*) "Act" phase – maintaining and improving the ISMS

3.. ISO/IEC 15408 (Evaluation Criteria for IT Security)

The international standard ISO/IEC 15408 is commonly known as the "Common Criteria" (CC). It consists of three parts:

ISO/IEC 15408-1:2005 (introduction and general model),

ISO/IEC 15408-2:2005 (security functional requirements)

ISO/IEC 15408-3:2005 (security assurance requirements).

This standard helps evaluate, validate, and certify the security assurance of a technology product against a number of factors, such as the security functional requirements specified in the standard.

4. ISO/IEC 13335 (IT Security Management)

ISO/IEC standard. It consists of a series of guidelines for technical security control measures:

(*a*) ISO/IEC 13335-1:2004 documents the concepts and models for information and communications technology security management.

(*b*) ISO/IEC TR 13335-3:1998 documents the techniques for the management of IT security. This is under review and may be superseded by ISO/IEC 27005.

(c) ISO/IEC TR 13335-4:2000 covers the selection of safeguards (i.e. technical security controls). This is under review and may be superseded by ISO/IEC 27005.

(d) ISO/IEC TR 13335-5:2001 covers management guidance on network security. This is also under review, and may be merged into ISO/IEC 18028-1, and ISO/IEC 27033.

PAYMENT CARD INDUSTRY DATA SECURITY STANDARD

The Payment Card Industry (PCI) Data Security Standard (DSS) 16 was developed by a number of major credit card companies as members of the PCI Standards Council to enhance payment account data security.

These requirements are organised into the following areas:

1. Build and Maintain a Secure Network

2. Protect Cardholder Data

3. Maintain a Vulnerability Management Program

4. Implement Strong Access Control Measures

COBIT

The Control Objectives for Information and related Technology (COBIT) is "a control framework that links IT initiatives to business requirements, organises IT activities into a generally accepted process model, identifies the major IT resources to be leveraged and defines the management control objectives to be considered.

Questions

Q.1. What are intellectual property and Intellectual Property Rights? What different categories of Intellectual properties have been define in India?

Q.2. Explain the features of Indian Copyright Act in details?

Q.3. What are the measures taken to secure data backup? What are the methods apply in order to secure backup?

Q.4. Explain Patent in details?

Q.5. Explain ISO Standard for information security in details?

Q.6. What are the use policy for information security explain it?

Q.7. Explain the patents, patentable inventions and non patentable inventions?

Chapter 14

CORPORATE POLICY

All companies should develop and maintain clear and robust policies for safeguarding critical business data and sensitive information, protecting their reputation and discouraging inappropriate behavior by employees.

Policy Development and Management

Many types of policies already exist for "real world" situations, but may need to be tailored to your organization and updated to reflect the increasing impact of cyberspace on everyday transactions, both professional and personal. As with any other business document, cyber security policies should follow good design and governance practices — not so long that they become unusable, not so vague that they become meaningless and reviewed on a regular basis to ensure that they stay pertinent as your business needs change.

Cyber Plan

1. Establish security roles and responsibilities

Clearly identify company data ownership and employee roles for security oversight and their inherit privileges, including:

- Necessary roles, and the privileges and constraints accorded to those roles.
- The types of employees who should be allowed to assume the various roles.
- How long an employee may hold a role before access rights must be reviewed.
- If employees may hold multiple roles, the circumstances defining when to adopt one role over another.

2. Establish an employee Internet usage policy

- Personal breaks to surf the web should be limited to a reasonable amount of time and to certain types of activities.

- If you use a web filtering system, employees should have clear knowledge of how and why their web activities will be monitored, and what types of sites are deemed unacceptable by your policy.

- Workplace rules of behavior should be clear, concise and easy to follow. Employees should feel comfortable.

- performing both personal and professional tasks online without making judgment calls as to what may or may not be deemed appropriate. Businesses may want to include a splash warning upon network sign-on that advises the employees of the businesses' Internet usage policies so that all employees are on notice.

3. Establish a social media policy

A strong social media policy is crucial for any business that seeks to use social networking to promote its activities and communicate with its customers. At a minimum, a social media policy should clearly include the following:

- Specific guidance on when to disclose company activities using social media, and what kinds of details can be discussed in a public forum.

- Additional rules of behavior for employees using personal social networking accounts to make clear what kinds of discussion topics or posts could cause risk for the company.

- Guidance on the acceptability of using a company email address to register for, or get notices from, social media sites.

- Guidance on selecting long and strong passwords for social networking accounts, since very few social media sites enforce strong authentication policies for users.

4. Identify potential reputation risks

All organizations should take the time to identify potential risks to their reputation and develop a strategy to mitigate those risks via policies or other measures as available. Specific types of reputation risks include:

- Being impersonated online by a criminal organization (e.g., an illegitimate website spoofing your business

- name and copying your site design, then attempting to defraud potential customers via phishing scams or other method).

- Having sensitive company or customer information leaked to the public via the web.

- Having sensitive or inappropriate employee actions made public via the web or social media sites.

Scams and Fraud

New telecommunication technologies may offer countless opportunities for small businesses, but they also offer cyber criminals many new ways to victimize your business, scam your customers and hurt your reputation. Businesses of all sizes should be aware of the most common scams perpetrated online.

Cyber Plan

1. Train employees to recognize social engineering

Social engineering, also known as "pretexting," is used by many criminals, both online and off, to trick unsuspecting people into giving away their personal information and/or installing malicious software onto their computers, devices or networks. Social engineering is successful because the bad guys are doing their best to make their work look and sound legitimate, sometimes even helpful, which makes it easier to deceive users.

Many criminals use social engineering tactics to get individuals to voluntarily install malicious computer software such as fake antivirus, thinking they are doing something that will help make them more secure. Users who are tricked into loading malicious programs on their computers may be providing remote control capabilities to an attacker, unwittingly installing software that can steal financial information or simply try to sell them fake security software.

2. Protect against online fraud

Online fraud takes on many guises that can impact everyone, including small businesses and their employees. It is helpful to maintain consistent and predictable online messaging when communicating with your customers to prevent others from impersonating your company.

3. Protect against phishing

Phishing is the technique used by online criminals to trick people into thinking they are dealing with a trusted website or other entity. Small businesses face this threat from two directions — phishers may be impersonating them to take advantage of unsuspecting customers, and phishers may be trying to steal their employees' online credentials.

4. Don't fall for fake antivirus offers

Fake antivirus, "scareware" and other rogue online security scams have been behind some of the most successful online frauds in recent times. Make sure your organization has a policy in place explaining what the procedure is if an employee's computer becomes infected by a virus.

5. Protect against malware

Businesses can experience a compromise through the introduction of malicious software, or malware, that tracks a user's keyboard strokes, also known as key logging. Many businesses are falling victim to key-logging malware being installed on computer systems in their environment. Once installed, the malware can record keystrokes made on a computer, allowing bad guys to see passwords, credit card numbers and other confidential data. Keeping security software up to date and patching your computers regularly will make it more difficult for this type of malware to infiltrate your network.

6. Verify the identify of telephone information seekers

Most offline social engineering occurs over the telephone. Information gathered through social networks and information posted on websites can be enough to create a convincing ruse to trick your employees. Ensure that you train employees to never disclose customer information, usernames, passwords or other sensitive details to incoming callers. When someone requests information, always contact the person back using a known phone number or email account to verify the identity and validity of the individual and their request.

Network Security

Securing your company's network consists of:

(1) identifying all devices and connections on the network.

(2) setting boundaries between your company's systems and others; and (3) enforcing controls to ensure that unauthorized access, misuse, or denial-of-service events can be thwarted or rapidly contained and recovered from if they do occur.

Cyber Plan

1. Secure internal network and cloud services

Your company's network should be separated from the public Internet by strong user authentication mechanisms and policy enforcement systems such as firewalls and web filtering proxies. Additional monitoring and security solutions, such as anti-virus software and intrusion detection systems, should also be employed to identify and stop malicious code or unauthorized access attempts.

Internal network

After identifying the boundary points on your company's network, each boundary should be evaluated to determine what types of security controls are necessary and how they can be best deployed. Border routers should be configured to only route traffic to and from your company's public IP addresses, firewalls should be deployed to restrict traffic only to and from the minimum set of necessary services, and intrusion prevention systems should be configured to monitor for suspicious activity crossing your network perimeter.

Cloud based services

Carefully consult your terms of service with all cloud service providers to ensure that your company's information and activities are protected with the same degree of security you would intend to provide on your own. Request security and auditing from your cloud service providers as applicable to your company's needs and concerns.

2. Develop strong password policies

Password policies should encourage your employees to employ the strongest passwords possible without creating the need or temptation to reuse passwords or write them down. That means passwords that are random, complex and long (at least 10 characters), that are changed regularly, and that are closely guarded by those who know them.

3. Secure and encrypt your company's Wi-Fi

Due to demonstrable security flaws known to exist in older forms of wireless encryption, your company's internal WLAN should only employ Wi-Fi Protected Access 2 (WPA2) encryption.

4. Encrypt sensitive company data

Encryption should be employed to protect any data that your company considers sensitive, in addition to meeting applicable regulatory requirements on information safeguarding. Different encryption schemes are appropriate under different circumstances.

5. Regularly update all applications

All systems and software, including networking equipment, should be updated in a timely fashion as patches and firmware upgrades become available.

6. Set safe web browsing rules

Your company's internal network should only be able to access those services and resources on the Internet that are essential to the business and the needs of your employees. Use the safe browsing features included with modern web browsing software and a web proxy to ensure that malicious or unauthorized sites cannot be accessed from your internal network.

Website Security

Website security is more important than ever. Web servers, which host the data and other content available to your customers on the Internet, are often the most targeted and attacked components of a company's network. Cyber criminals are constantly looking for improperly secured websites to attack, while many customers say website security is a top consideration when they choose to shop online. As a result, it is essential to secure servers and the network infrastructure that supports them. The consequences of a security breach are great: loss of revenues, damage to credibility, legal liability and loss of customer trust.

The following are examples of specific security threats to web servers:

- Sensitive unencrypted information transmitted between the web server and the browser may be intercepted.

- Information on the web server may be changed for malicious purposes. Website defacement is a commonly reported example of this threat.

- Cyber criminals may gain unauthorized access to resources elsewhere in the organization's network via a successful attack on the web server.

Cyber Plan

1. Carefully plan and address the security aspects of the deployment of a public web server.

Businesses also need to consider the human resource requirements for the deployment and continued operation of the web server and supporting infrastructure. The following points in a deployment plan:

- Types of personnel required — for example, system and web server administrators, webmasters, network administrators and information systems security personnel.

- Skills and training required by assigned personnel.

- Individual (i.e., the level of effort required of specific personnel types) and collective staffing (i.e., overall level of effort) requirements.

2. Implement appropriate security management practices and controls when maintaining and operating a secure web server.

Appropriate management practices are essential to operating and maintaining a secure web server The following practices and controls are recommended:

- A business-wide information system security policy.
- Server configuration and change control and management.
- Risk assessment and management.
- Standardized software configurations that satisfy the information system security policy.
- Security awareness and training.

3. Ensure that web server operating systems meet your organization's security requirements.

Initially securing an operating system initially generally includes the following steps:

- Patch and upgrade the operating system.
- Change all default passwords

- Remove or disable unnecessary services and applications.
- Configure operating system user authentication.
- Configure resource controls.
- Install and configure additional security controls

4. Ensure the web server application meets your organization's security requirements.

Securing the web server application generally includes the following steps:

- Patch and upgrade the web server application.
- Remove or disable unnecessary services, applications and sample content.
- Configure web server user authentication and access controls.
- Configure web server resource controls.

5. Ensure that only appropriate content is published on your website.

Company websites are often one of the first places cyber criminals search for valuable information. Still, many businesses lack a web publishing process or policy that determines what type of information to publish openly, what information to publish with restricted access and what information should not be published to any publicly accessible repository. Some generally accepted examples of what should not be published or at least should be carefully examined and reviewed before being published on a public website include:

- Classified or proprietary business information.
- Sensitive information relating to your business' security.
- Medical records.
- A business' detailed physical and information security safeguards.
- Details about a business' network and information system infrastructure — for example, address ranges, naming conventions and access numbers.
- Information that specifies or implies physical security vulnerabilities.
- Detailed plans, maps, diagrams, aerial photographs and architectural drawings of business buildings, properties or installations
- Any sensitive information about individuals that might be subject to federal, state or, in some instances, international privacy laws.

6. Ensure appropriate steps are taken to protect web content from unauthorized access or modification.

Although information available on public websites is intended to be public (assuming a credible review process and policy is in place), it is still important to ensure that information cannot be modified without authorization. Users of such information rely on its integrity even if the information is not confidential. Content on publicly accessible web servers is inherently more vulnerable than information that is inaccessible from the Internet, and this vulnerability means businesses need to protect public web content through the appropriate configuration of web server resource controls. Examples of resource control practices include:

- Install or enable only necessary services.
- Install web content on a dedicated hard drive or logical partition.
- Limit uploads to directories that are not readable by the web server.
- Define a single directory for all external scripts or programs executed as part of web content.
- Disable the use of hard or symbolic links.
- Define a complete web content access matrix identifying which folders and files in the web server document directory are restricted, which are accessible, and by whom.
- Disable directory listings.
- Deploy user authentication to identify approved users, digital signatures and other cryptographic mechanisms as appropriate.
- Use intrusion detection systems, intrusion prevention systems and file integrity checkers to spot intrusions and verify web content.

7. Use active content judiciously after balancing the benefits and risks.

Static information resided on the servers of most early websites, typically in the form of text-based documents. Soon thereafter, interactive elements were introduced to offer new opportunities for user interaction. Unfortunately, these same interactive elements introduced new web-related vulnerabilities. They typically involve dynamically executing code using a large number of inputs, from web page URL parameters to hypertext transfer protocol (HTTP) content and, more recently, extensible markup language (XML) content. Different active content technologies pose different related vulnerabilities, and their risks should be weighed against their benefits. Although most websites use some form of active content generators, many also deliver some or all of their content in a static form.

8. Use authentication and cryptographic technologies as appropriate to protect certain types of sensitive data.

Public web servers often support technologies for identifying and authenticating users with differing privileges for accessing information. Some of these technologies are based on cryptographic functions that can provide a secure channel between a web browser client and a web server that supports encryption. Web servers may be configured to use different cryptographic algorithms, providing varying levels of security and performance.

Without proper user authentication in place, businesses cannot selectively restrict access to specific information. All information that resides on a public web server is then accessible by anyone with access to the server. In addition, without some process to authenticate the server, users of the public web server will not be able to determine whether the server is the "authentic" web server or a counterfeit version operated by a cyber criminal.

9. Employ network infrastructure to help protect public web servers.

The network infrastructure (e.g., firewalls, routers, intrusion detection systems) that supports the web server plays a critical security role. In most configurations, the network infrastructure will be the first line of defense between a public web server and the Internet. Network design alone, though, cannot protect a web server. The frequency, sophistication and variety of web server attacks perpetrated today support the idea that web server security must be implemented through layered and diverse protection mechanisms, an approach sometimes referred to as "defense-indepth."

10. Commit to an ongoing process of maintaining web server security.

Maintaining a secure web server requires constant effort, resources and vigilance. Securely administering a web server on a daily basis is essential. Maintaining the security of a web server will usually involve the following steps:

- Configuring, protecting and analyzing log files.
- Backing up critical information frequently.
- Maintaining a protected authoritative copy of your organization's web content.
- Establishing and following procedures for recovering from compromise.
- Testing and applying patches in a timely manner.
- Testing security periodically.

Email

Email has become a critical part of our everyday business, from internal management to direct customer support. The benefits associated with email as a primary business tool far outweigh the negatives. However, businesses must be mindful that a successful email platform starts with basic principles of email security to ensure the privacy and protection of customer and business information.

Cyber Plan

1. Set up a spam email filter

It has been well documented that spam, phishing attempts and otherwise unsolicited and unwelcome email often accounts for more than 60 percent of all email that an individual or business receives. Email is the primary method for spreading viruses and malware and it is one of the easiest to defend against. Consider using email-filtering services that your email service, hosting provider or other cloud providers offer. A local email filter application is also an important component of a solid antivirus strategy. Ensure that automatic updates are enabled on your email application, email filter and anti-virus programs. Ensure that filters are reviewed regularly so that important email and/or domains are not blocked in error.

2. Train your employees in responsible email usage

The last line of defense for all of your cyber risk efforts lies with the employees who use tools such as email and their responsible and appropriate use and management of the information under their control. Technology alone cannot make a business secure. Employees must be trained to identify risks associated with email use, how and when to use email appropriate to their work, and when to seek assistance of professionals. Employee awareness training is available in many forms, including printed media, videos and online training.

3. Protect sensitive information sent via email

With its proliferation as a primary tool to communicate internally and externally, business email often includes sensitive information. Whether it is company information that could harm your business or regulated data such as personal health information (PHI) or personally identifiable information (PII), it is important to ensure that such information is only sent and accessed by those who are entitled to see it.

4. Set a sensible email retention policy

Another important consideration is the management of email that resides on company messaging systems and your users' computers. From the cost of storage and backup to legal and regulatory requirements, companies should document how they will handle email retention and implement basic controls to help them attain those standards. Many industries have specific rules that dictate how long emails can or should be retained, but the basic rule of thumb is only as long as it supports your business efforts. Many companies implement a 60-90 day retention standard if not compelled by law to another retention period.

5. Develop an email usage policy

Policies are important for setting expectations with your employees or users, and for developing standards to ensure adherence to your published polices.

\Your policies should be easy to read, understand, define and enforce. Key areas to address include what the company email system should and should not be used for, and what data are allowed to be transmitted. Other policy areas should address retention, privacy and acceptable use.

Questions

Q.1. What is Corporate Policy, Explain in details?

Q.2. Explain in details Policy Development and management?

Q.3. What are the use of cyber plan in poilicy development?

Q.4. What are the use of cyber plan in Network Security?

Q.5. What are the use of cyber plan in Website Security?

Q.6. What are the use of cyber plan in E-mail?

1. ....means, the information should be available only to those who are authorized to access:

   (*a*) **Availability**   (*b*) Integrity

   (*c*) Confidentiality   (*d*) None of the above

2. The following is an attempt to trick an audience into believing that something false is real

   (*a*) **Hoax**   (*b*) Identity Theft

   (*c*) Phishing   (*d*) Virus

3. Is an attempt to make a computer unavailable to its intended users:

   (*a*) Social Networking   (*b*) **Denial of Service**

   (*c*) Identity Theft   (*d*) None of the above

4. That pretend to be helpful programs while destroying your data, damaging your computer, and stealing your personal information.

   (*a*) Virus   (*b*) Spyware

   (*c*) **Trojan**   (*d*) Social Engineering

5. A Computer is called as .... computer which is connected to internet and controlled by hacker by inserting the malicious software and used to perform attacks

   (*a*) Malicious computer   (*b*) **Botnet**

   (*c*) Zombie   (*d*) None of the above

6. Prevention of unauthorized disclosure of Information is called as:

   (*a*) Availability   (*b*) **Confidentiality**

   (*c*) Integrity   (*d*) Authenticity

7. **E-mail sent by online criminals to trick you into going to fake Web sites and revealing personal information is termed as:**

   (*a*)   Identity Theft   (*b*)   Spam

   (*c*)   **Phishing**   (*d*)   Virus

8. **The following happenswhen a criminal tries to take over another person's account**

   (*a*)   Account Takeover   (*b*)   Application Fraud

   (*c*)   **Both (a) & (b)**   (*d*)   None of the above

9. **It is an art of convincing the people to reveal the confidential information**

   (*a*)   Denial of Service   (***b***)   **Social Engineering**

   (*c*)   Spam   (*d*)   None of the above

10. **WWW is**

    (***a***)   **Internet-based global information system**

    (*b*)   LAN based information system

    (*c*)   Intranet-based global information system

    (*d*)   None of the above

11. **http://www.yahoo.com is**

    (*a*)   Website address   (*b*)   URL address

    (*c*)   E-mail address   (***d***)   **Both a & b**

12. **Interruption is**

    (*a*)   Identity theft   (**b**)   **Unavailability of data**

    (*c*)   Denial of Service   (d)   All of the above

13. **Safety tips for public computer usage**

    (*a*)   Not to save log-on information

    (*b*)   Erase tracks

    (*c*)   Enable the feature that stores passwords

    (***d***)   **Both a and b**

14. **HTTP is an application**

    (*a*)   a web server to web browser

    (*b*)   a file server to web browser

    (*c*)   both a and b

    (***d***)   **None of the above**

15. The following is not an Internet search engine

- (*a*) Google
- (*b*) Webcrawler
- (*c*) **Adobe Pagemaker**
- (*d*) Excite

16. Pretty good privacy (PGP) is used in

- (*a*) browser security
- (***b***) **email security**
- (*c*) FTP security
- (*d*) none of the mentioned

17. PGP encrypts data by using a block cipher called

- (***a***) **international data encryption algorithm**
- (*b*) private data encryption algorithm
- (*c*) intrenet data encryption algorithm
- (*d*) none of the mentioned

18. An attempt to make a computer resource unavailable to its intended users is called

- (***a***) **denial-of-service attack**
- (*b*) virus attack
- (*c*) worms attack
- (*d*) botnet process

19. WPA2 is used for security in

- (*a*) ethernet
- (*b*) bluetooth
- (***c***) **wi-fi**
- (*d*) none of the mentioned

20. In computer security, ... means that computer system assets can be modified only by authorized parities.

- (*a*) Confidentiality
- (***b***) **Integrity**
- (*c*) Availability
- (*d*) Authenticity

21. In computer security, ... means that the information in a computer system only be accessible for reading by authorized parities.

- (***a***) **Confidentiality**
- (*b*) Integrity
- (*c*) Availability
- (*D*) Authenticity

22. The type of threats on the security of a computer system or network are ....

- (*i*) Interruption
- (*ii*) Interception
- (*iii*) Modification
- (*iv*) Creation
- (*v*) Fabrication

- (*a*) i, ii, iii and iv only
- (*b*) ii, iii, iv and v only
- (***c***) **i, ii, iii and v only**
- (*d*) All i, ii, iii, iv and v

23. Which of the following is independent malicious program that need not any host program?

    (*a*) Trap doors   (*b*) Trojan horse

    (*c*) Virus   **(*d*) Worm**

24. Ths .... is code that recognizes some special sequence of input or is triggered by being run   from a certain user ID of by unli............kely sequence of events.

    (*a*) Trap doors   (*b*) Trojan horse

    (*c*) Logic Bomb   (*d*) Virus

25. The .... is code embedded in some legitimate program that is set to "explode" when certain conditions are met.

    (*a*) Trap doors   (*b*) Trojan horse

    (*c*) Logic Bomb   (*d*) Virus

26. Which of the following malicious program do not replicate automatically?

    (*a*) Trojan Horse   (*b*) Virus

    (*c*) Worm   (*d*) Zombie

27. .... programs can be used to accomplish functions indirectly that an unauthorized user could not accomplish directly.

    (*a*) Zombie   (*b*) Worm

    (*c*) Trojan Horses   (*d*) Logic Bomb

28. State whether true of false.

    (*i*) A worm mails a copy of itself to other systems.

    (*ii*) A worm executes a copy of itself on another system.

    (*a*) True, False   (*b*) False, True

    (*c*) True, True   (*d*) False, False

29. A .... is a program that can infect other programs by modifying them, the modification includes a copy of the virus program, which can go on to infect other programs.

    (*a*) Worm   **(*b*) Virus**

    (*c*) Zombie   (*d*) Trap doors

30. 2 are used in denial of service attacks, typically against targeted web sites.

    (*a*) Worm   **(*b*) Zombie**

    (*c*) Virus   (*d*) Trojan horse

31. Select the correct order for the different phases of virus execution.

    (*i*) Propagation phase   (*ii*) Dormant phase

    (*iii*) Execution phase   (*iv*) Triggering phase

    (*a*)   i, ii, iii, and iv   (*b*) i, iii, ii and iv

    (*c*) ii, i, iv an iii   (*d*) ii, iii, iv and i

32. **A .... attaches itself to executable files and replicates, when the infected program is executed, by finding other executable files to infect.**

    (*a*) Stealth virus   (*b*) Polymorphic Virus

    (*c*) Parasitic Virus   (*d*) Macro Virus

33. **............ is a form of virus explicitly designed to hide itself from detection by antivirus software.**

    (*a*) *Stealth virus*   (*b*) Polymorphic Virus

    (*c*) Parasitic Virus   (*d*) Macro Virus

34. **A .... creates copies duringreplication that are functionally equivalent but have distinctly different bit patterns.**

    (*a*) Boot Sector Virus   **(*b*) Polymorphic Virus**

    (*c*) Parasitic Virus   (*d*) Macro Virus

35. **A portion of the Polymorphic virus, generally called a ...., creates, a random encryption, key to encrypt the remainder of the virus.**

    (a) mutual engine   **(*b*) mutation engine**

    (*c*) multiple engine   (*d*) polymorphic engine

36. **State whether the following statement is true.**

    (*i*) A macro virus is platform independent.

    (*ii*) Macro viruses infect documents, not executable portions of code.

    (*a*) i-only   (*b*) ii-only

    (*c*) Both i and ii   (*d*) Non i and ii

37. **The type(s) of auto executing macros, in Microsoft word is/are**

    (*a*) Auto execute   (*b*) Auto macro

    (*c*) Command macro   **(*d*) All of the above**

38. **In .... ,the virus places an identical copy of itself into other programs or into certain system areas on the disk.**

    (*a*) Dormant phase   **(*b*) Propagation phase**

    (*c*) Triggering phase   (*d*) Execution phase

39. **A .... is a program that secretly takes over another Internet-attached computer and then uses that computer to launch attacks.**

    (*a*) Worm   **(*b*) Zombie**

    (*c*) Virus   (d) Trap doors

40. **This is a class of programs that searches your hard drive and floppy disks for any known or potential viruses.**

    (*a*) intrusion detection   (*b*) security identifier

    (*c*) Antigen   (***d***) **antivirus software**

41. **What is the name for a program or programming code that replicates by being copied or initiating its copying to another program, computer boot sector or document?**

    (*a*) Spyware   (***b***) **Virus**

    (*c*) Firewall.   (*d*) Norton.

42. **Which is a good choice in this situation?**

"If someone from your bank calls you and asks you to update your personal information including bank account number and social security number you will"

    (*a*) Give all the information as it is good for my bank to have my updated information.

    (*b*) Just give social security number, the bank should know your account number already.

    (*c*) Give bank account number and other details except social security number.

    (***d***) **Offer to visit the nearest branch and update as required or call the bank with the number you know is authentic.**

43. **You receive an email from an unknown source asking you to download a patch that will make your computer more secure. You will**

    (*a*) download the patch and not forward to anyone.

    (*b*) download, install and burn it on a cd as backup for future use.

    (*c*) download the patch and forward the email to all your friends to help them.

    (***d***) **ignore, report as spam and delete the email.**

44. **Someone from a charity calls and asks you for a donation over the phone and you want to donate money. What will you do?**

    (*a*) Give credit card or bank account information over the phone to donate money.

    (***b***) **Request the caller to mail information to you by post so you can research about them before donating.**

    (*c*) Ask them a postal address and mail them a check.

45. **You have a Mac so you don't have to worry about viruses.**

    (***a***) **False**   (*b*) True

46. **Windows XP Professional with SP2 is COMPLETELY secure.**

    (*a*) True   (***b***) **False**

47. **The next time you order checks, you will do this for security reasons:**

    (*a*) Your social security number printed near your name.

    (*b*) Have only your initials (instead of first name) and last name put on them.

48. **How can you prevent intruders from accessing your wireless network?**

    (*a*) Encrypt network traffic with WPA or WEP

    (*b*) Restrict access to trusted MAC addresses

    (*c*) Both

49. **You receive an email that claims that if you forward the email to 15 of your friends you will get lucky otherwise you will have bad luck for the next few months. What will you do?**

    (*a*) You will forward the email.

    (b) Ignore and just delete the email.

50. **What governs the type of traffic that is and is not allowed through a firewall?**

(***a***) **rule base**	(*b*) gateway
(*c*) access control list	(*d*) partition

51. **What is the term for an attempt to determine the valid e-mail addresses associated with an e-mail server so that they can be added to a spam database?**

(*a*) X-mail harvest	(***b***) **Directory harvest attack**
(*c*) Spambot attack	(*d*) Email validator

52. **What protocol ensures privacy between communicating applications and their users on the Internet?**

(*a*) F-Secure	(b) Privacy Control Protocol
(*c*) Secure Shell Authentication	(***d***) **Transport Layer Security**

53. **This standard being developed by IBM, Microsoft, Novell and others will allow different manufacturers' biometric software to interact.**

(*a*) IDEA	(*b*) Twofish
(*c*) **BioAPI**	

54. **This two-level scheme for authenticating network users functions as part of the Web's Hypertext Transfer Protocol.**

(*a*) SSL	(*b*) CRAM
(*c*) **LUHN formula**	

55. **This standard being developed by IBM, Microsoft, Novell and others will allow different manufacturers' biometric software to interact.**

(*a*) IDEA	(*b*) Twofish
(*c*) **BioAPI**	

56. **What is the term for an attempt to determine the valid e-mail addresses associated with an e-mail server so that they can be added to a spam database?**

   (*a*)   X-mail harvest   (*b*)   **Directory harvest attack**

   (*c*)   Spambot attack   (*d*)   Email validator

57. **What governs the type of traffic that is and is not allowed through a firewall?**

   (*a*)   **rule base**   (b)   gateway

   (*c*)   access control list   (*d*)   partition

58. **This two-level scheme for authenticating network users functions as part of the Web's Hypertext Transfer Protocol.**

   (*a*)   SSL   B.   **CRAM**

   (c)   LUHN formula

59. **What protocol ensures privacy between communicating applications and their users on the Internet?**

   (a)   F-Secure   (*b*)   Privacy Control Protocol

   (*c*)   Secure Shell Authentication   (*d*)   **Transport Layer Security**

60. **This is a common type of denial-of-service attack that involves sending more traffic to a network address than the temporary data storage area is intended to hold, thereby shutting down the service and possibly corrupting or overwriting valid data**

   (*a*)   war dialing   (*b*)   **buffer overflow**

   (*c*)   smurf attack   (*d*)   bucket brigade

61. **Microsoft's Passport is an example of this technology, which allows users to register their personal information once to access multiple applications.**

   (*a*)   Microsoft Point-to-Point Encryption.

   (*b*)   **Single Signon.**

   (c)   Relative Identifier.

   (d)   Biometric Verification

62. **Anti Virus programs protect your computer from spyware.**

   (a)   True   (*b*)   **False**

63. **This is a computer system on the Internet that is expressly set up to attract and "trap" intruders.**

   (*a*)   Exploit   (*b*)   demilitarized zone

   (*c*)   Trojan horse   (*d*)   **honeypot**

64. **Your friend sends you a website link requesting you to update your address information. What will you do?**

   (*a*)   Click on the link and update the information.

   (*b*)   **Read the privacy policy on the website and decide if you want to provide the information or not.**

   (*c*)   Update and forward the link to all your friends.

   (*d*)   Report your friends email address as spam.

65. **Which of the following methods does spyware use to install on an end user's machine?**

   (*a*)   Bundling with free peer-to-peer programs

   (*b*)   Social engineering

   (*c*)   Search toolbars

   (*d*)   **All of the above**

66. **WEP i a security protocol, specified in 802.11b, that is designed to provide a wireless local area network (WLAN) with a level of security and privacy comparable to what is usually expected of a wired LAN. What does WEP stand for?**

   (*a*)   **Wired Equivalent Privacy**

   (*b*)   Wireless Equivalent Protocol

   (*c*)   Wireless Equivalent Privacy

67. **Firewall is a software or hardware that can protect a computer from virus.**

   (*a*)   **False**   (*b*)   True

68. **While you were browsing the web, you get a pop up window that says "Congratulations! You just won a TV, click here to claim". You ...**

   (*a*)   feel very happy, click on it and give all the information it asks.

   (*b*)   **just close the window and ignore it.**

69. **Windows XP is secure by default**

   (*a*)   **False**   (*b*)   True

70. **What do you call a program used to detect unsolicited and unwanted e-mail and prevents those messages from getting to a user's inbox?4**

   (*a*)   anti-spammer.   (*b*)   email guard.

   (*c*)   virus filter.   (*d*)   **spam filter.**

71. **You receive an email from an unknown source asking you to download a patch that will make your computer more secure. You will**

   (*a*)   download the patch and forward the email to all your friends

   (*b*)   download the patch and not forward to anyone.

    (*c*)   **ignore, report as spam and delete the email.**

    (*d*)   download, install and burn it on a cd as backup for future use.

72. HTTPS is a Web protocol developed by Netscape and built into its browser that encrypts and decrypts user page requests as well as the pages that are returned by the Web server. What does HTTPS stand for?

    (*a*) Hypertext Transfer Protocol Security

    (*b*) Hypertext Transfer Protocol over Secure Socket Layer

    (*c*) Hypertext Transfer Protocol over Sublayer

73. What is SSL used for?

    (*a*)   Encrypt data as it travels over a network

    (*b*)   Encrypt passwords for storage in a database

    (*c*)   Encrypt files located on a Web server

    (*d*)   Encrypt digital certificates used to authenticate a Web site

74. In order to protect yourself from identity theft you should

    (*a*)   Order and review your credit report from the credit reporting bureaus at least once a year.

    (*b*)   Never give personal information over the phone such as social security number or financial information unless you initiated the phone call.

    (*c*)   Review your credit card statements and bank statements for discrepancies.

    (*d*)   All of the above.

75. How does spyware differ from other forms of malware, such as worms and viruses?

    (*a*)   The delivery mechanism is unaware that it contains spyware.

    (*b*)   Spyware installs without the user's knowledge.

    (*c*)   Not all spyware is malicious.

    (*d*)   Spyware replicates itself.

76. Phishing and Pharming are forms of social engineering.

    (*a*) True   (b) False

77. Once you have logged on to your bank's website you can determine that SSL is being used on the site by looking for

    (*a*)   A small padlock icon, usually in the lower right corner of your Web browser window. A closed, or locked padlock indicates a secure connection.

    (*b*)   https:// — in the address line of your browser.

    (*c*)   Both

78. On average, how long does it take for an unprotected networked computer to be compromised once it is connected to the internet?

    (*a*) 1 Week

    (***b***) **20 minutes**

    (*c*) 10 hours

    (*d*) 7 Days

79. What type of attack relies on the trusting nature of employees and the art of deception?

    (***a***) **Social Engineering**

    (*b*) Fraud

    (*c*) Phishing

    (*d*) Dumpster Diving

80. You may give someone your password if:

    (***a***) **It is never OK to give out your password**

    (*b*) Your Boss asks you for your password

    (*c*) The helpdesk asks you for your password

    (*d*) Your Boss says it is OK to give someone your password

81. What can a firewall protect against?

    (*a*) Viruses

    (***b***) **Unauthenticated interactive logins from the outside world**

    (*c*) Fire

    (*d*) Connecting to and from the outside world

82. The National Security Alliance in 2004 estimated what percentage of home PCs are infected with spyware?

    (*a*) 20%

    (*b*) 40%

    (*c*) 60%

    (***d***) **80%**

83. In comparison to the illegal drug trade, Cyber crime generates:

    (*a*) Less Money

    (*b*) It is mainly done by computer geeks for kicks instead of money

    (***c***) **More Money**

84. This is a document that states in writing how a company plans to protect the company's physical and IT assets.

    (*a*) Data Encryption Standard

    (***b***) **Security policy**

    (*c*) Public key certificate

    (*d*) Access control list

85. This is a program or file that is specifically developed for the purpose of doing harm:

    (*a*) Buffer overflow

    (*b*) Bastion host

    (***c***) **Malware**

    (*d*) Ping sweep

86. **This is a program in which malicious or harmful code is contained inside apparently harmless programming or data.**

    A.   War dialer   (*b*) Spam trap

    C.   **Trojan horse**   (*d*) Email

87. **What are the three most important things you can do to secure desktop PCs?**

    (*a*) Turn on Automatic Updates   (*b*) Turn on Windows Firewall

    (*c*) Install anti-virus software   (*d*) Remove the hard drive

    A.   a, c, and d

    (*b*) **a, b, and c**   (*c*) b, c, and d

    (*d*) a, b, and d   (*e*) only c

88. **Which of the following is an example of a strong password?**

    (*a*) Password

    (*b*) **J*p2le04>F**   (*c*) Your real name, user name, or company name

89. **True of false: If you set your anti-virus software to auto-update then you don't need Windows Automatic Updates.**

    (*a*) True   (*b*) **False**

90. **What is "phishing?"**

    (*a*) **"Spoofed" e-mails and fraudulent websites designed to fool recipients into divulging personal financial data such as credit card numbers, account usernames and passwords**

    (*b*) A type of computer virus

    (*c*) An example of a strong password

    (*d*) A boring activity that uses a rod and bait.

    (*e*) None of the above

91. **You receive an e-mail message from someone you know well with Subject: line 'Here it is' and the file attachment is named draft.doc. What do you do?**

    (*a*) Open the attachment

    (*b*) Save the attachment to disk and scan it for viruses

    (*c*) **Contact the sender to determine if he/she created and sent the draft.doc attachment**

92. **You are using e-mail to send and receive private information (e.g. medical data, salary information, social security numbers, passwords). What do you do?**

    (*a*) Put all of the information in one large message before sending it to reduce the chance that it will fall into the wrong hands

    (*b*) **Encrypt the information before sending it through e-mail**

    (*c*)   Put the information in many small messages so that only a small information will be exposed if it falls into the wrong hands.

93. You are receiving bothersome or threatening e-mail messages. What do you do?

    (*a*)   Save the messages and report the problem to your supervisor

    (*b*)   Ignore the messages and delete them

    (*c*)   Contact the police

    (*d*).   Hire a hit man to rough them up

94. You learn about a new screen saver that you can download from the Internet to put on your PC at work. What do you do?

    (*a*)   Don't download the screen saver. This action is not allowed.

    (*b*)   Download the screen saver and scan it for viruses before installing it.

    (*c*)   Search the Internet for reports describing this screen saver.

95. You get a new computer. What do you do?

    A.   Connect it to the network and start using it.

    B.   Secure it against the most common attacks, connect it to the network and start using it.

    C.   Don't connect it to the network.

96. According to the FBI and the Computer Security Institute, most information security breaches occur due to what?

    (*a*)   External Hackers   (*b*)   Poor Programming

    (*c*)   Internal Employees   (*d*)   Bad Firewall Settings

97. Which of the following is the most important to install and keep up to date on your personal computer?

    (*a*)   Anti-virus and anti-spyware software

    (*b*)   Anti-spam software

    (*c*)   A Firewall

    (*d*)   Operating system updates

    (*e*)   All of the above must be installed and kept up to date

98. What percentage of people have reported that someone has stolen personally-identifiable information?

    (*a*)   5%   B.   10%

    C.   15%   D.   20%

    E.   25%

99. **Typo-squatting is?**

    (*a*)   A typo in operating system code that gives malware easy entry

    (*b*)   A malicious website using a URL similar to a real one

    (*c*)   The process of patching vulnerabilities

    (*d*)   What online grammar-police complain about

100. .... **programs can be used to accomplish functions indirectly that an unauthorized user could not accomplish directly.**

    (*a*)   Zombie   (*b*)   Worm

    (*c*)   Trojan Horses   (*d*)   Logic Bomb

Q.1 **What are the security threats in Social Networking?**

Ans: (*i*) Personal information stealing

(*ii*) Session Hijacking

(*1*) It reveals your location.

Q.2 **What are the laws present in India to ensure Cyber Security?**

Ans: Information Security Act.

Q.3 **In country where even the President get threatening mails, how secure are internet facilities?**

Ans: Not secure. But awareness helps.

Q.4 **Is there some agency acting as regulatory body?**

Ans: Internet is unregulated. There are advisory and organisation help in mitigating cyber threat.

Q.5 **What is information security?**

Ans: Information security in today's enterprise is a "well-informed sense of assurance that the information risks and controls are in balance."

- The protection of information and its critical elements, including the systems and hardware that use, store, and transmit that information

- Tools, such as policy, awareness, training, education, and technology are necessary

Q.6 **What is C.I.A?**

Ans: The C.I.A. triangle was the standard based on confidentiality, integrity, and availability. The C.I.A. triangle has expanded into a list of critical characteristics of information

Q.7 **Write a note on the history of information security**

Ans: • Computer security began immediately after the first mainframes were developed

- Groups developing code-breaking computations during World War II created the first modern computers

- Physical controls were needed to limit access to authorized personnel to sensitive military locations

- Only rudimentary controls were available to defend against physical theft, espionage, and sabotage

Q.8 **What is the scope of computer security?**

Ans: The scope of computer security grew from physical security to include:

a. Safety of the data

b. Limiting unauthorized access to that data

c. Involvement of personnel from multiple levels of the organization

Q.9   What is Security?

Ans: • "The quality or state of being secure—to be free from danger"

   • To be protected from adversaries

Q.10. Define Physical security

Ans: Physical Security – to protect physical items, objects or areas of organization from unauthorized access and misuse. Protect the physical asset.

Q.11. Define Personal Security?

Ans: Personal Security involves protection of individuals or group of individuals who are authorized to access the organization and its operations.

Q.12. Define Operations security

Ans: Operations security focuses on the protection of the details of particular operations or series of activities. It handles with the resources of the organization.

Q.13. Define Communications security

Ans: Communications security – encompasses the protection of organization's communications media, technology and content.

Q.14. Define Network security

Ans: Network security – is the protection of networking components, connections, and contents

Q.15. Define Information security

Ans: Information security – is the protection of information and its critical elements, including the systems and hardware that use , store, and transmit the information

Q.16. What are the critical characteristics of information?

Ans: 1. Availability   2. Accuracy ?   3. Authenticity   4. Confidentiality   5. Integrity 6. Procession

Q.17. What is NSTISSC Security model?

Ans: • This refers to "The National Security Telecommunications and Information Systems Security.

   • Committee" document. This document presents a comprehensive model for information security.

   • The model consists of three dimensions.

Q.18. What are the components of an information system?

Ans: An Information System (IS) is much more than computer hardware; it is the entire set of software, hardware, data, people, and procedures necessary to use information as a resource in the organization.

Q.19. What is meant by balancing Security and Access?

Ans: Balancing Security and Access

   It is impossible to obtain perfect security - it is not an absolute; it is a process ?

To achieve balance, the level of security must allow reasonable access, yet protect against threats ?

Security should be considered a balance between protection and availability

Q.20. What are the approaches used for implementing information security?

Ans: Bottom Up Approach ?

Top-down Approach ?

Q.21. What is SDLC?

Ans: The Systems Development Life Cycle

- Information security must be managed in a manner similar to any other major system implemented in the organization
- Using a methodology
- ensures a rigorous process ?
- avoids missing steps ?

Q.22. What is Security SDLC?

Ans: Security Systems Development Life Cycle

The same phases used in the traditional SDLC adapted to support the specialized implementation of a security project

Basic process is identification of threats and controls to counter them

The SDLC is a coherent program rather than a series of random, seemingly unconnected actions

Q.23. What are threats?

Ans:
- A threat is an object, person, or other entity that represents a constant danger to an asset
- Management must be informed of the various kinds of threats facing the organization

  By examining each threat category in turn, management effectively Protects its information through policy, education and training, and technology controls.

Q.24. What is Intellectual property?

Ans: Intellectual property is "the ownership of ideas and control over the tangible or virtual representation of those ideas". Many organizations are in business to create intellectual property

Q.25. Who are Hackers? What are the two hacker levels?

Ans: The classic perpetrator of deliberate acts of espionage or trespass is the hacker. Hackers are "people who use and create computer software [to] gain access to information illegally".

Generally two skill levels among hackers:

- Expert hacker
- unskilled hacker(Script kiddies)

Q.26. What is information extortion?

Ans: • Information extortion is an attacker or formerly trusted insider stealing information from a computer system and demanding compensation for its return or non-use ?

• Extortion found in credit card number theft(A Russian hacker named Maxus, who hacked the online vendor and stole everal hundred thousand credit card numbers.

Q.27. What is Cyber terrorism?

Ans: Cyber terrorism is amost sinister form of hacking involving cyber terrorists hacking

Systems to conduct terrorist activities through network or internet pathways.

An example was defacement of NATO web pages during the war in Kosovo.

Q.28. What are deliberate software attacks?

Ans: When an individual or group designs software to attack systems, they create malicious

code/software called malware

Designed to damage, destroy, or deny service to the target systems Includes:

macro virus

boot virus

worms

Trojan horses

logic bombs

back door or trap door

denial-of-service attacks

polymorphic

Q.29. What are technical hardware failures or errors?

Ans: • Technical hardware failures or errors occur when a manufacturer distributes to users equipment containing flaws

• These defects can cause the system to perform outside of expected parameters, resulting in unreliable service or lack of availability

• Some errors are terminal, in that they result in the unrecoverable loss of the equipment

• Some errors are intermittent, in that they only periodically? manifest themselves, resulting in faults that are not easily repeated

Q.30. What are technical software failures or errors?

Ans: • This category of threats comes from purchasing software with unrevealed faults

• Large quantities of computer code are written, debugged, published, and sold onlyto determine that not all bugs were resolved

• Sometimes, unique combinations of certain software and hardware reveal new bugs

• Sometimes, these items aren't errors, but are purposeful shortcuts left by programmers for honest or dishonest reasons

Q.31. What is an attack?

Ans: An attack is the deliberate act that exploits vulnerability

It is accomplished by a threat-agent to damage or steal an organization's information or physical asset ?
An exploit is a technique to compromise a system

A vulnerability is an identified weakness of a controlled system whose controls are not present or are no longer effective

An attack is then the use of an exploit to achieve the compromise of a controlled system

Q.32. What is a malicious code?

Ans: This kind of attack includes the execution of viruses, worms, Trojan horses, and active web scripts with the intent to destroy or steal information. The state of the art in attacking systems in 2002 is the multi-vector worm using up to six attack vectors to exploit a variety of vulnerabilities in commonly found information system devices.

Q.33. What is Distributed Denial-of-service (DDoS)?

Ans: D-DoS is an attack in which a coordinated stream of requests is launched against a target from many locations at the same time.

Q.34. Define Dictionary attack

Ans: The dictionary password attack narrows the field by selecting specific accounts to attack and uses a list of commonly used passwords (the dictionary) to guide guesses.

Q.35. What are the various forms of attacks?

Ans:
- IP Scan and Attack
- Web Browsing
- Virus
- Unprotected Shares
- Mass Mail
- SNMP
- Hoaxes
- Back Doors
- Password Crack
- Brute Force
- Dictionary

Q.36. What is Denial-of-service (DoS) ?

Ans:
1. attacker sends a large number of connection or information requests to a target
2. so many requests are made that the target system cannot handle them successfully

along with other, legitimate requests for service

3. may result in a system crash, or merely an inability to perform ordinary functions

Q.37. Define Spoofing

Ans: It is a technique used to gain unauthorized access whereby the intruder sends messages to a computer with an IP address indicating that the message is coming from a trusted host.

Q.38. Define Man-in-the-Middle

Ans: Man-in-the-middle is an attacker sniffs packets from the network, modifies them, and inserts them back into the network.

Q.39. What is risk management?

Ans: Risk management is the process of identifying vulnerabilities in an organization's information systems and taking carefully reasoned steps to assure

- Confidentiality
- Integrity
- Availability of all the components in the organization's information systems

Q.40. What the roles to be played by the communities of interest to manage the risks an organization encounters?

Ans: It is the responsibility of each community of interest to manage risks; each community has a role to play:

- Information Security
- Management and Users
- Information Technology

Q.41. What is the process of Risk Identification?

1. A risk management strategy calls on us to "know ourselves" by identifying, classifying, and prioritizing the organization's information assets
2. These assets are the targets of various threats and threat agents and our goal is to protect them from these threats.

Q.42. What are asset identification and valuation?

Ans: This iterative process begins with the identification of assets, including all of the elements of an organization's system: people, procedures, data and information, software, hardware, and networking elements.

Q.43. What is Asset Information for People?

Ans:
- Position name/number/ID
- Supervisor

- Security clearance level
- Special skills

Q.44. How information assets are classified?

Ans: Examples of these kinds of classifications are:

- confidential data
- internal data
- public data
- Informal organizations may have to organize themselves to create a useable data classification model
- The other side of the data classification scheme is the personnel security clearance structure

Q.45. Define the process of Information asset valuation.

Ans:
- Create a weighting for each category based on the answers to the previous questions
- Which factor is the most important to the organization?
- Once each question has been weighted, calculating the importance of each asset is straightforward.
- List the assets in order of importance using a weighted factor analysis worksheet.

Q.46. Explain the process of threat identification?

Ans: Threat Identification

- Each of the threats identified so far has the potential to attack any of the assets protected
- This will quickly become more complex and overwhelm the ability to plan
- To make this part of the process manageable, each step in the threat identification and vulnerability identification process is managed separately, and then coordinated at the end of the process

Q.47. How to identify and Prioritize Threats?

- Each threat must be further examined to assess its potential to impact organization - this is referred to as a threat assessment
- To frame the discussion of threat assessment, address each threat with a few questions:
- Which threats present a danger to this organization's assets in the given environment?
- Which threats represent the most danger to the organization's information?
- How much would it cost to recover from a successful attack?
- Which of these threats would require the greatest expenditure to prevent?

Q.48. What is Vulnerability Identification?

Ans:
- We now face the challenge of reviewing each information asset for each threat it faces and creating a list of the vulnerabilities that remain viable risks to the organization

- Vulnerabilities are specific avenues that threat agents can exploit to attack an information asset

- Examine how each of the threats that are possible or likely could be perpetrated and list the organization's assets and their vulnerabilities

- The process works best when groups of people with diverse backgrounds within the organization work iteratively in a series of brainstorming sessions

Q.49. Mention the Risk Identification Estimate Factors

Ans: • Likelihood ?

- Value of Information Assets

- Percent of Risk Mitigated

- Uncertainty

Q.50. Give an example of Risk determination.

For the purpose of relative risk assessment:

risk = likelihood of vulnerability occurrence times value (or impact) - percentage risk already controlled + an element of uncertainty Information Asset A has an value score of 50 and has one vulnerability:

- Vulnerability 1 has a likelihood of 1.0 with no current controls and you estimate that assumptions and data are 90 % accurate

   Asset A: vulnerability rated as $55 = (50 * 1.0) - 0\% + 10\%$

Q.51. What is residual risk?

- For each threat and its associated vulnerabilities that have any residual risk, create a preliminary list of control ideas

- Residual risk is the risk that remains to the information asset even after the existing control has been applied

Q.52. What is access control?

Ans: One particular application of controls is in the area of access controls

- Access controls are those controls that specifically address admission of a user into a trusted area of the organization

- There are a number of approaches to controlling access

- Access controls can be - discretionary , mandatory , nondiscretionary

Q.53. What are the different types of Access Controls?

Ans: • Discretionary Access Controls (DAC)

- Mandatory Access Controls (MACs)

- Nondiscretionary Controls

- Role-Based Controls
- Task-Based Controls
- Lattice-based Control

Q.54. What is the goal of documenting results of the risk assessment?

Ans:
- The goal of this process has been to identify the information assets of the organization that have specific vulnerabilities and create a list of them, ranked for focus on those most needing protection first
- In preparing this list we have collected and preserved factual information about the assets, the threats they face, and the vulnerabilities they experience

Q.55. What are the different risk control strategies?

Ans:
- Avoidance
- Transference
  - Mitigation
  - Acceptance

Q.56. Define Disaster Recovery Plan

Ans: The most common mitigation procedure is Disaster Recovery Plan(DRP). The DRP includes the entire spectrum of activities used to recover from the incident and strategies to limit losses before and after the disaster. DRP usually include all preparations for the recovery process, strategies to limit losses during the disaster.

Q.57. What is a policy?

Ans: A policy is a plan or course of action, as of a government, political party, or business, intended to influence and determine decisions, actions, and other matters.

Q.58. What are the three types of security policies?

Ans: Management defines three types of security policy:
- General or security program policy
- Issue-specific security policies
- Systems-specific security policies

Q.59. What is Security Program Policy?

Ans: A security program policy (SPP) is also known as
- A general security policy
- IT security policy
- Information security policy

Q.60. Define Issue-Specific Security Policy (ISSP)

Ans: The ISSP:

- addresses specific areas of technology
- requires frequent updates
- contains an issue statement on the organization's position on an issue

Q.61. What are ACL Policies?

Ans: ACLs allow configuration to restrict access from anyone and anywhere

ACLs regulate:

- Who can use the system?
- What authorized users can access?
- When authorized users can access the system?
- Where authorized users can access the system from?
- How authorized users can access the system?

Q.62. What is Information Security Blueprint?

Ans: The Security Blue Print is the basis for Design, Selection and Implementation of Security Policies, education and training programs, and technology controls.

Q.63. Define ISO 17799/BS 7799 Standards and their drawbacks

One of the most widely referenced and often discussed security? models is the Information Technology – Code of Practice for Information Security Management, which was originally published as British Standard BS 7799

This Code of Practice was adopted as an international standard by? the International Organization for Standardization (ISO) and the International Electrotechnical Commission (IEC) as ISO/IEC 17799 in 2000 as a framework for information security

Q.64. What are the objectives of ISO 17799?

Organizational Security Policy is needed to provide management direction and support Objectives:

- Operational Security Policy
- Organizational Security Infrastructure
- Asset Classification and Control
- Personnel Security
- Physical and Environmental Security
- Communications and Operations Management
- System Access Control
- System Development and Maintenance
- Business Continuity Planning
- Compliance ?

Q.65. **List the management controls of NIST SP 800-26**

- Risk Management ?

- Review of Security Controls ?

- Life Cycle Maintenance

- Authorization of Processing (Certification and Accreditation) ?

Q.66. **Mention the Operational Controls of NIST SP 800-26**

Ans: • Personnel Security ?

- Physical Security

- Production, Input/output Controls

- Contingency Planning

- Hardware and Systems Software

- Data Integrity

- Documentation

- Security Awareness, Training, and Education

- Incident Response Capability

Q.67. What is Sphere of protection?

Ans: The "sphere of protection" overlays each of the levels of the? "sphere of use" with a layer of security, protecting that layer from direct or indirect use through the next layer

The people must become a layer of security, a human firewall that protects the information from unauthorized access and use

Information security is therefore designed and implemented in three layers

- policies ?

- people (education, training, and awareness programs) ?

Q.68. What is Security perimeter?

Ans: • The point at which an organization's security protection?ends, and the outside world begins is referred to as the security perimeter

Q.69. What is Systems-Specific Policy (SysSP)?

Ans: • SysSPs are frequently codified? as standards and procedures used when configuring or maintaining systems

- Systems-specific policies fall into two groups: ?

- Access control lists (ACLs) consist of the access control lists,? matrices, and capability? tables governing the rights and privileges of a particular user to a particular system

Q.70. What is the importance of blueprint?

Ans: The blueprint should specify the tasks to be accomplished and the order in which they are to be realized. It should serve as a scaleable, upgradable, and comprehensive plan for the information security needs for coming years.

Q.71. What are the approaches of ISSP?

Ans: Three approaches:

- Create a number of independent ISSP documents ?
- Create a single comprehensive ISSP document ?
- Create a modular ISSP document

Q.72. What are firewalls?

Ans: A firewall is any device that prevents a specific type of information from moving between the untrusted network outside and the trusted network inside

The firewall may be:

- a separate computer system ?
- a service running on an existing router or server ?
- a separate network containing a number of supporting devices

Q.73. Explain different generations of firewalls.

Ans:
- First Generation - packet filtering firewalls
- Second Generation-application-level firewall or proxy server
- Third Generation- Stateful inspection firewalls
- Fourth Generation-dynamic packet filtering firewall
- Fifth Generation- kernel proxy

Q.74. What are Screened-Host Firewall Systems

Ans: Screened-Host firewall system allows the router to pre-screen packets to minimize the network traffic and load on the internal proxy.

Q.75. What is the use of an Application proxy?

Ans: An Application proxy examines an application layer protocol, such as HTTP, and performs the proxy services

Q.76. What is Public Key Infrastructure (PKI)?

Ans: PKI or Public Key I2nfrastructure

- Public Key Infrastructure is the entire set of hardware, software, and cryptosystems necessary to implement public key encryption

    PKI systems are based on public-key cryptosystems and include digital certificates and certificate authorities (CAs) and can:

- Issue digital certificates
- Issue crypto keys

Q.77. How E-mail systems are secured?

Ans:
- Encryption cryptosystems have been adapted to inject some degree of security into e- mail:
- S/MIME builds on the Multipurpose Internet Mail Extensions (MIME) encoding format by

adding encryption and authentication

- Privacy Enhanced Mail (PEM) was proposed by the Internet Engineering Task Force (IETF) as a standard to function with the public key cryptosystems
- PEM uses 3DES symmetric key encryption and RSA for key exchanges and digital signatures
- Pretty Good Privacy (PGP) was developed by Phil Zimmerman and uses the IDEA Cipher along with RSA for key exchange

INDEX

SPECIAL BONUS!

Want These 3 Bonus Books for free?

Get <u>FREE</u>, unlimited access to these and all of our new books by joining our community!

SCAN w/ your camera TO JOIN!

OR Visit

freebie.kartbucket.com

www.ingramcontent.com/pod-product-compliance
Lightning Source LLC
Chambersburg PA
CBHW060113120726
48003CB00009B/2621